COMPOSITION AND PERSPECTIVE

A simple, yet powerful guide to draw stunning, expressive sketches

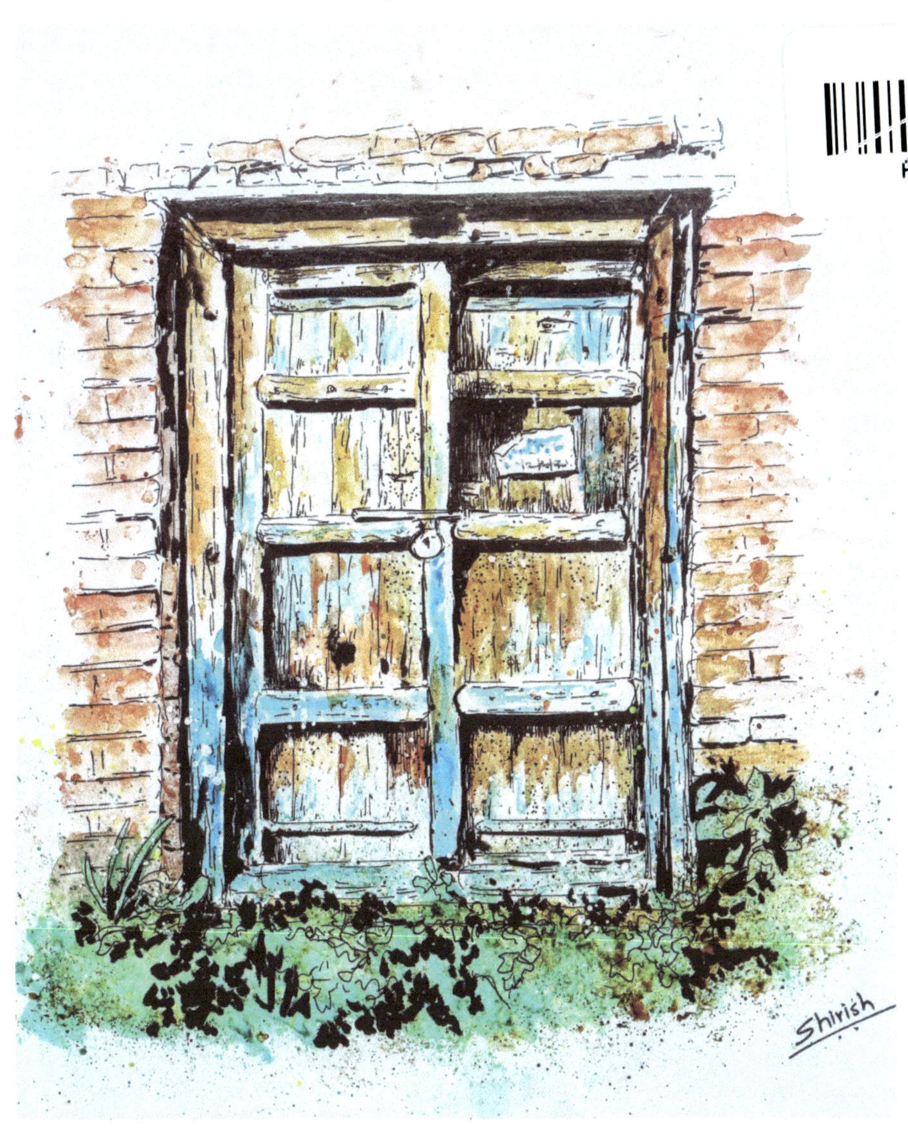

https://HuesAndTones.net

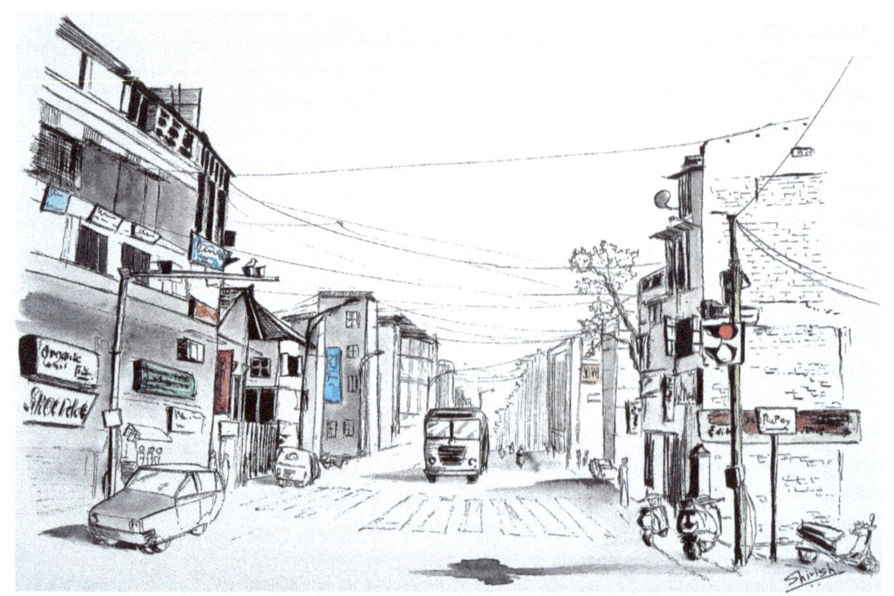

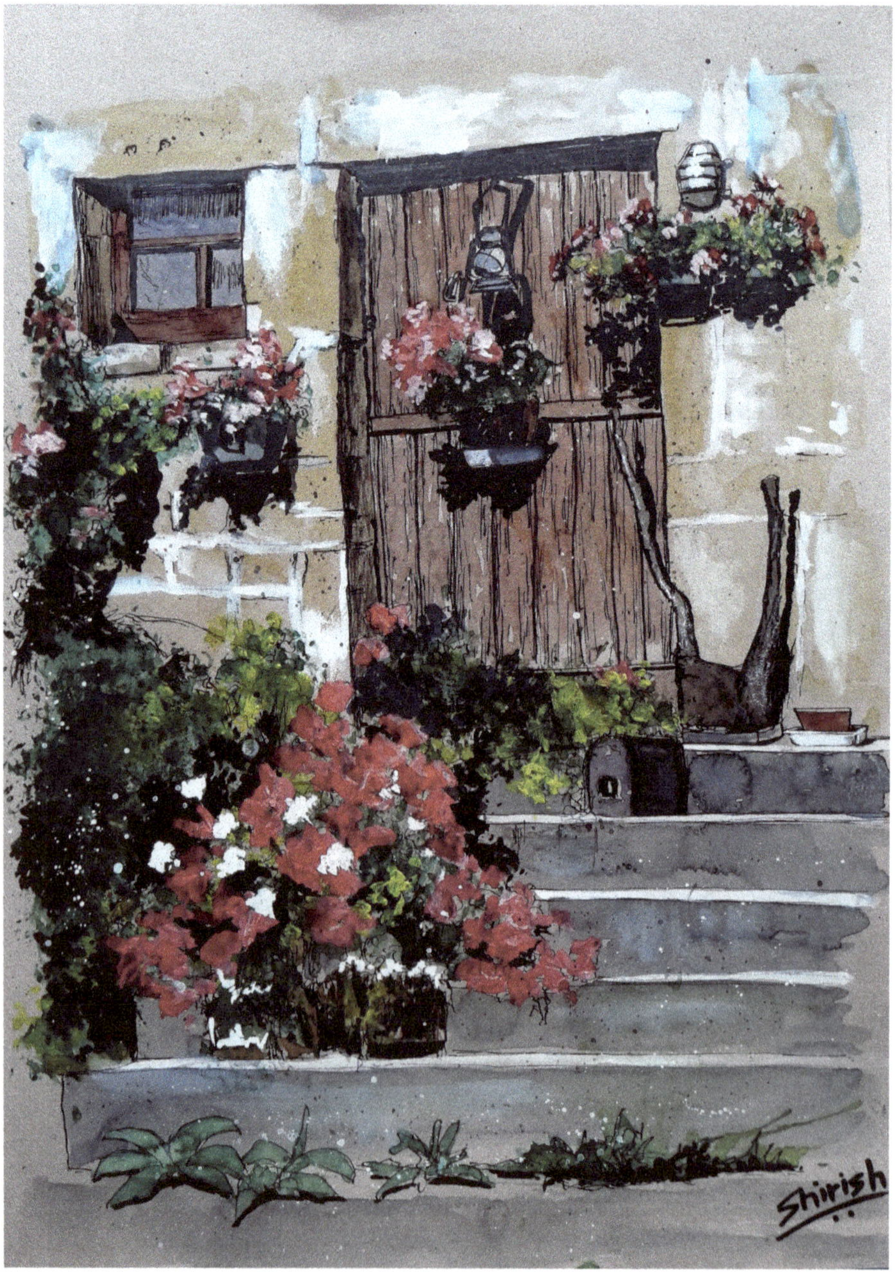

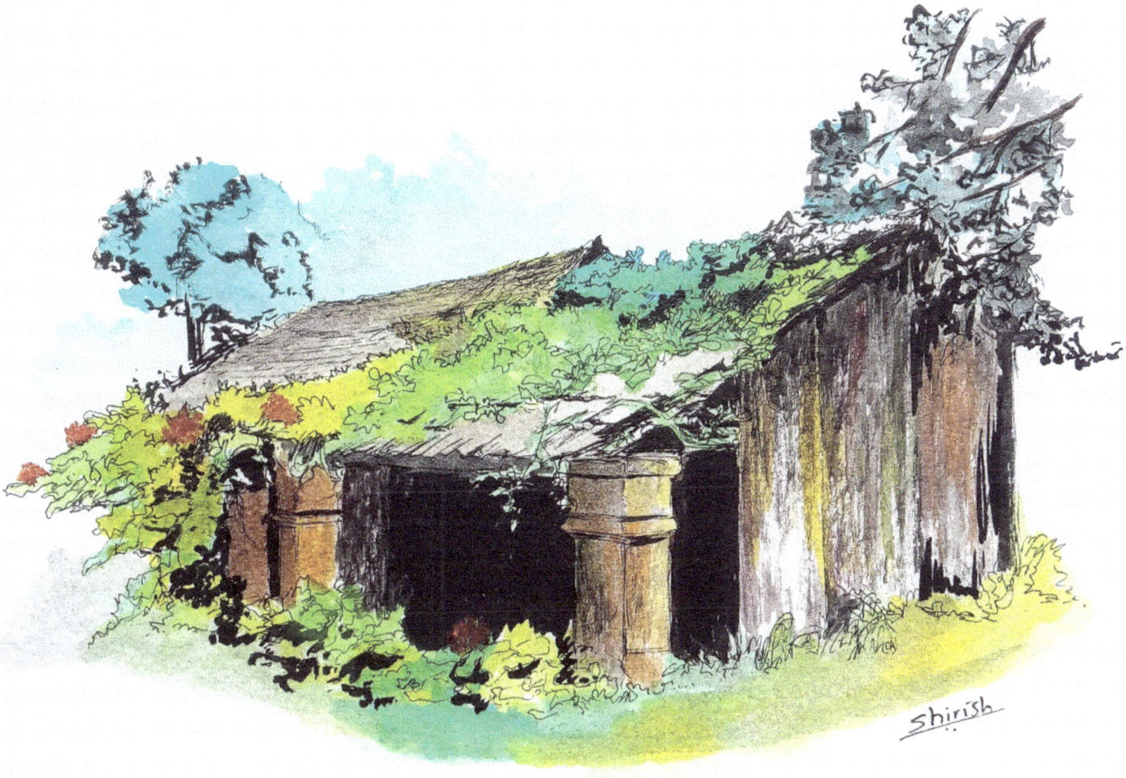

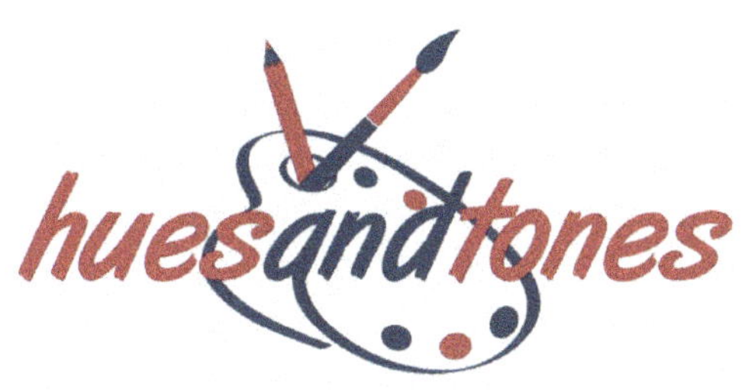

Copyright ©2018 by:

HueaAndTones Media and Publishing

Author: Shirish Deshpande

First edition

Table of Contents

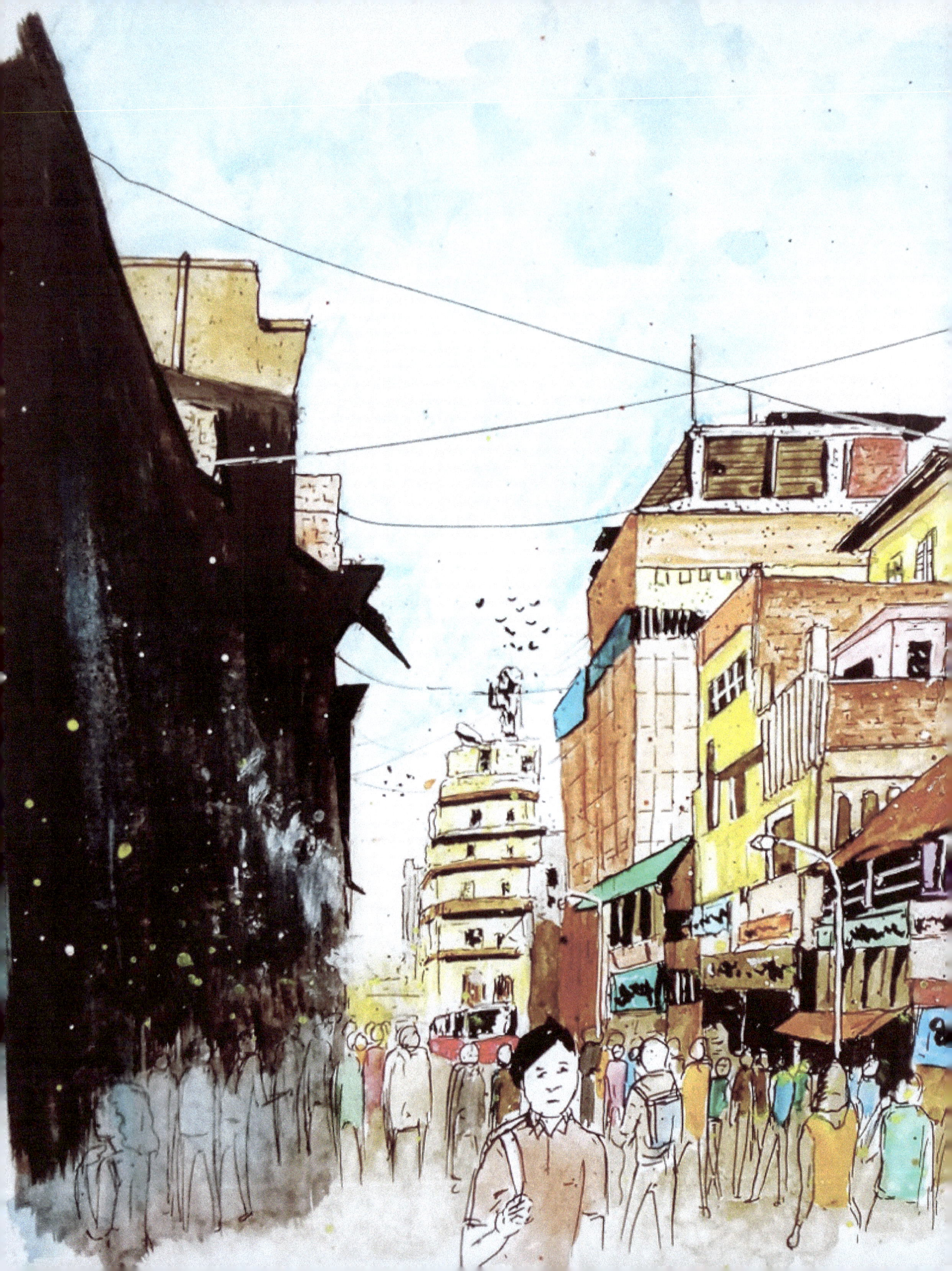

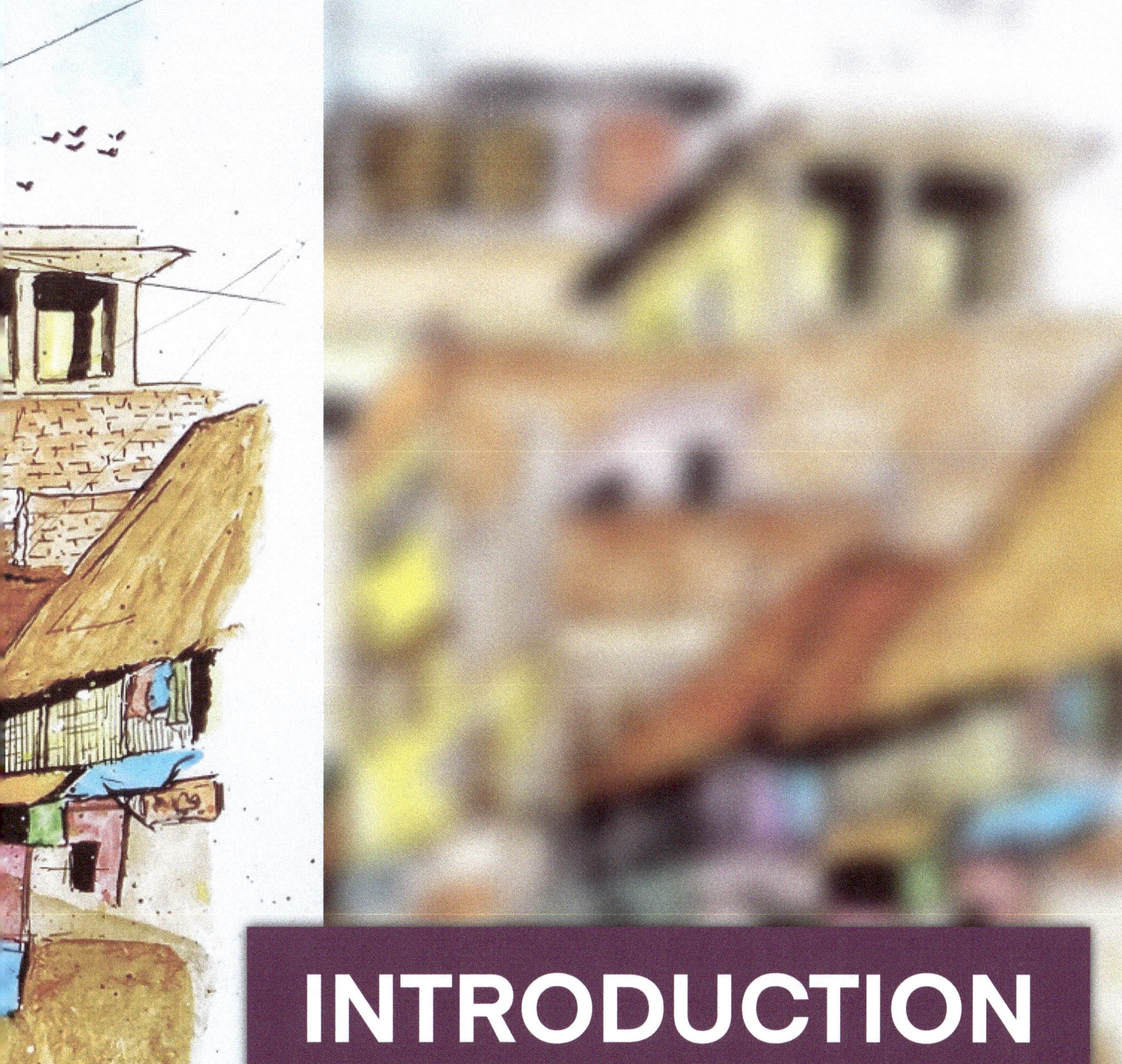

INTRODUCTION

Bonus: Want to see how the sketch on the previous page was sketched in all its colorful glory?

Then head over to the following URL:

https://tinyurl.com/y9q5gsqd

Alternatively, you may use the QR code given below to watch the complete video of the making of this sketch. And don't forget to subscribe to the channel!

A Note Before You Begin

Throughout this book, you will come across YouTube links below several artworks. These are marked as 'Bonus'. These links lead to the demonstration videos for the respective artworks.

Are you reading a paper version of this book (or an e-book version on an e-ink device)? Then typing all these links on a video-capable device like a phone/tab/PC may prove to be a bit tedious for you.

But no worries!

I have provided a QR code against each URL, which you can use to access the video contents.

Alternatively, you can directly head over to the web page mentioned below. This page contains the complete list of YouTube links in this book. Click on the artwork image for which you want to see the demonstration, and you will be redirected to the respective video.

And the best part? This bonus material is absolutely FREE!

Type the following URLs in your browser window (or use the QR code).

https://huesandtones.net/pages/cp-links/

Who Is This Book For?

The focus of this book is on sketching and painting. So, at first glance, it may seem that this book is only for the benefit of sketchers and painters.

But, the concepts of composition and perspective are universal. They apply to all kind of visual art.

Are you interested in any kind of visual art like sketching, painting, photography or film-making?

If yes, then there's something for you in this book.

But all the demonstrations mentioned in this book make use of pencils, pens, inks, and watercolors.

Throughout this book, I will compose the sentences related to composition and perspective from the perspective of sketching and painting!

But it will refer, in fact, to every kind of visual art.

What Is This Book About?

As it's often quoted in sports, 'Form is temporary, but class is permanent'.

Think of composition and perspective as the 'class' element in your visual art!

Composition and Perspective are the two elements which make or break a picture.

You may not even notice them when they are correctly present in a sketch. But you will notice them when they are not.

I have met many people who claim that they have no understanding of art. And yet, they can still notice when the perspective in a sketch is incorrect!

They may not understand precisely what is wrong. But they will definitely feel that something is wrong.

One more thing… this book will only discuss the 'realistic' kind of sketching/painting.

'Realistic' does not necessarily mean hyper-realistic or photorealistic. It means the sketches contain recognizable elements. In other words, we will not cover any abstract artworks in this book.

Stop Reading This Book Now...

If...

- You are looking to learn architectural perspective (with measurements and stuff).

- You are looking to learn photorealistic sketching/painting.

Architectural drawings are all about accuracy and proportions. While an artist does strive to mimic correct relative proportions in his/her artwork, it's not a necessity.

This book will focus purely on the 'expressive' style of sketching/painting, not on photorealism. But keep in mind that 'expressive' does not mean inaccurate!

The expressive artwork is about depicting the feel of an element/scene. It should still look believable. But the artist has the liberty to focus on the beauty and the grace of art. The mathematical accuracy is not that important.

Materials

I have used pencils, pens, inks, and watercolors to render most of the artworks in this book. Some are rendered using oil colors/acrylic colors/digital means.

All the YouTube videos mentioned in this book are done using pencils, pens, inks, and watercolors.

Practicing the concepts you will learn in this book, is non-negotiable. The concepts of composition and perspective should not be merely read, but be internalized. And for internalizing them, you will need to practice them. A lot.

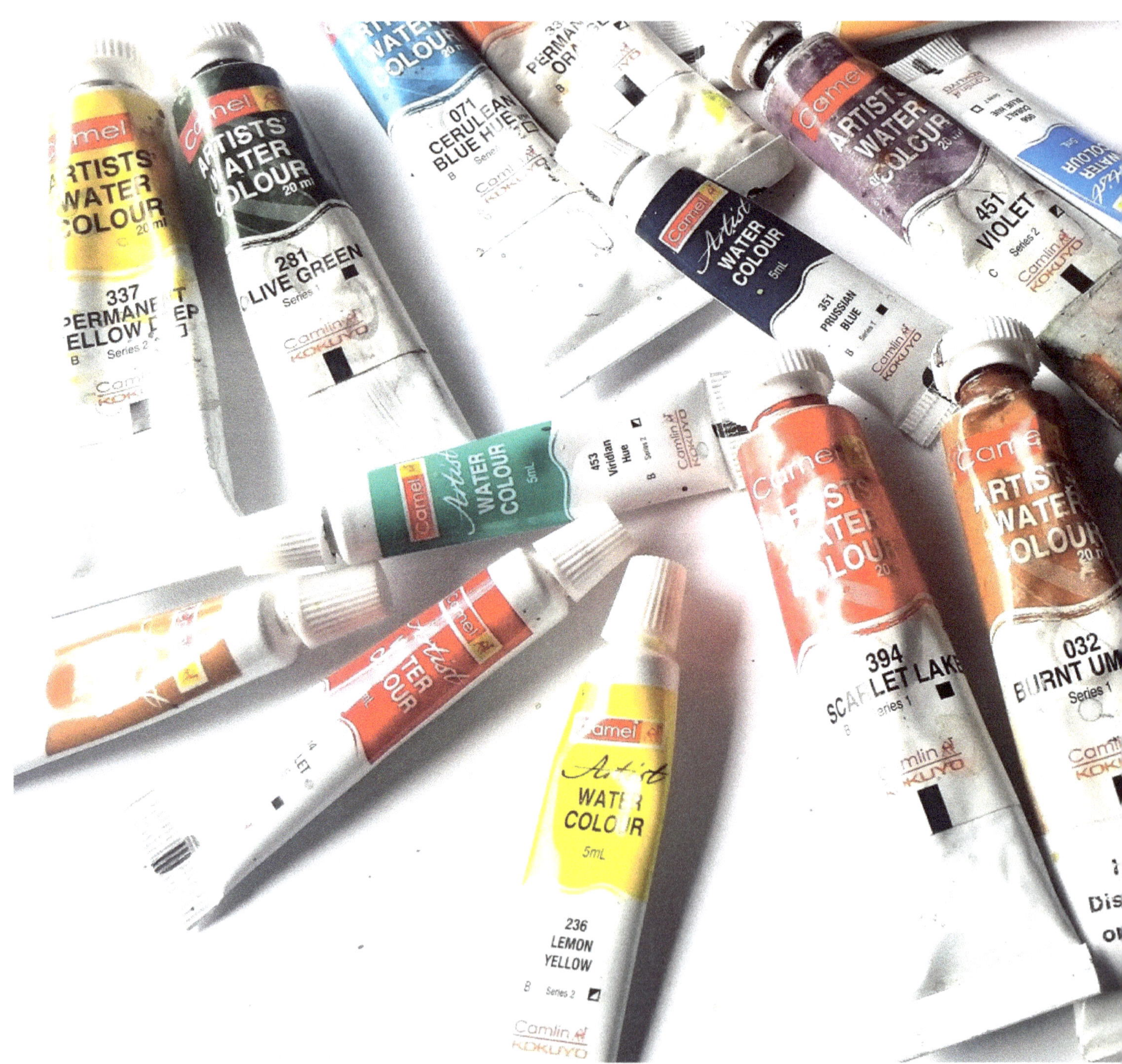

That's why I have included this chapter to discuss the materials. These materials can be used for rendering perspective sketches, and they will help you make better sense of the video demonstrations.

What I am going to discuss here are only guidelines based on the way I do things. You may use any materials as per your choice and comfort level for practicing. There's no need to strictly abide by what I do here.

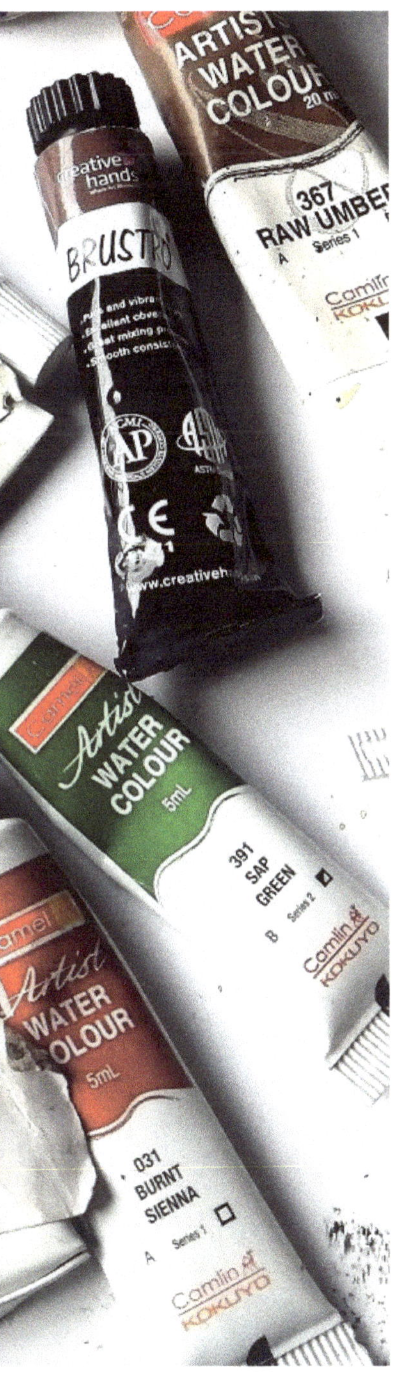

Do you want to learn sketching and painting using pens, inks, and watercolor? Then you may want to check out my other books here:

https://www.HuesAndTones.net/books/

There are no defined rules about the materials. But I have a few recommendations based on my experience.

Requirement: Perspective lines and rough sketching.

Material: Mechanical pencil (HB), Ruler (12'/30cm).

Paper specifications: Any sketch paper of 70 GSM or more.

Requirement: Pencil sketch.

Material: Mechanical pencil, soft lead pencil, ruler, eraser, sharpener.

Paper specifications: Any sketch paper of 70 GSM or more.

Requirement: Pen sketch.

Material: Mechanical pencil, ruler, eraser, sharpener, ballpoint pens/gel pens/ technical pens, brush pens.

Paper specifications: Any sketch paper of 70 GSM or more.

Requirement: Pen and inks and/or watercolors

Material: Same as that for pen sketch + inks, watercolors, watercolor brushes, soft tissues, water.

Paper specifications: Any sketch paper of 70 GSM or more. If doing a lot of wet work, use 250 GSM or above. If using pens, I will recommend hot pressed/ smooth papers. If using only watercolors/inks, handmade/cold pressed papers can also be used.

With that context set, let's dive into the first part… Composition!

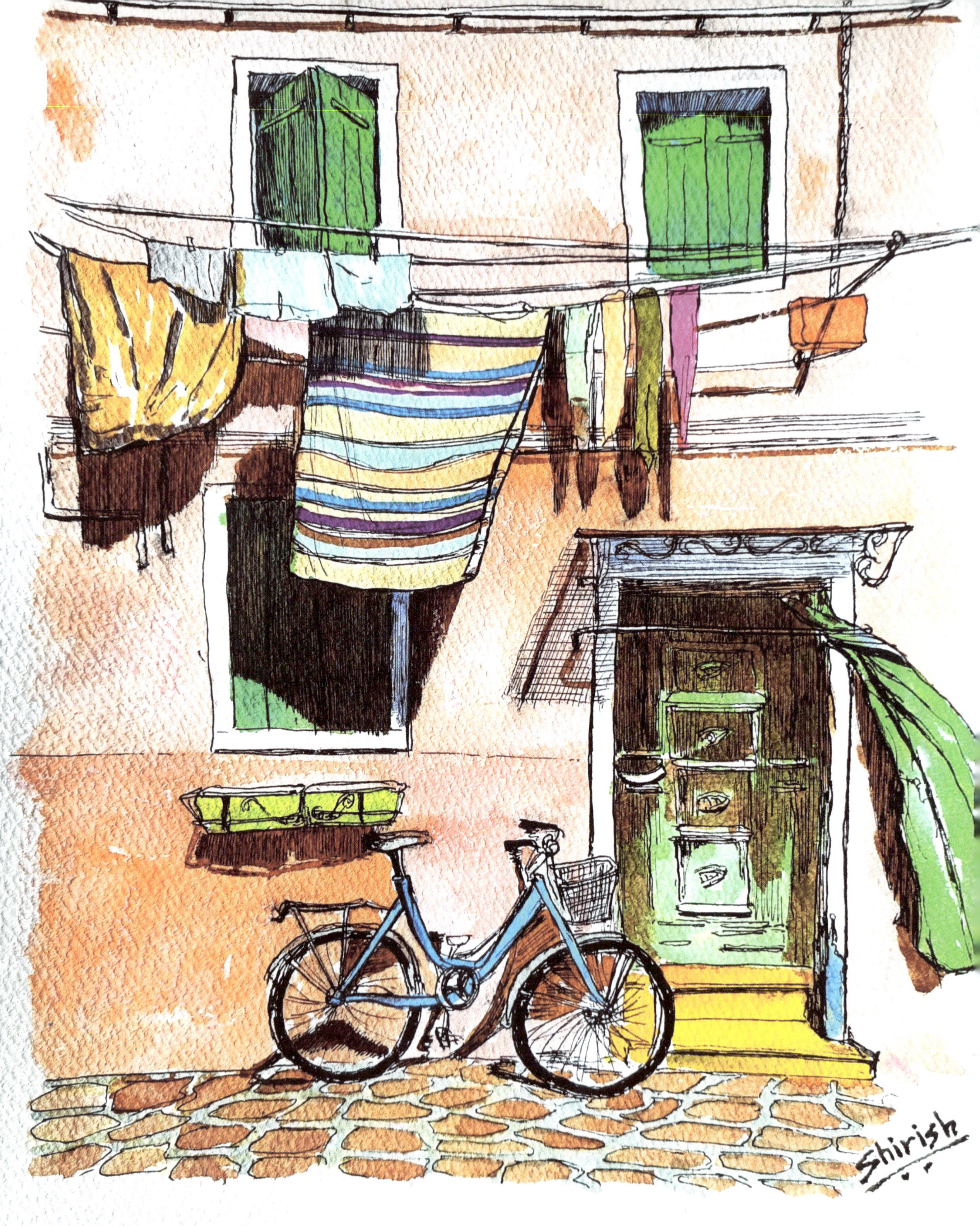

Shirish

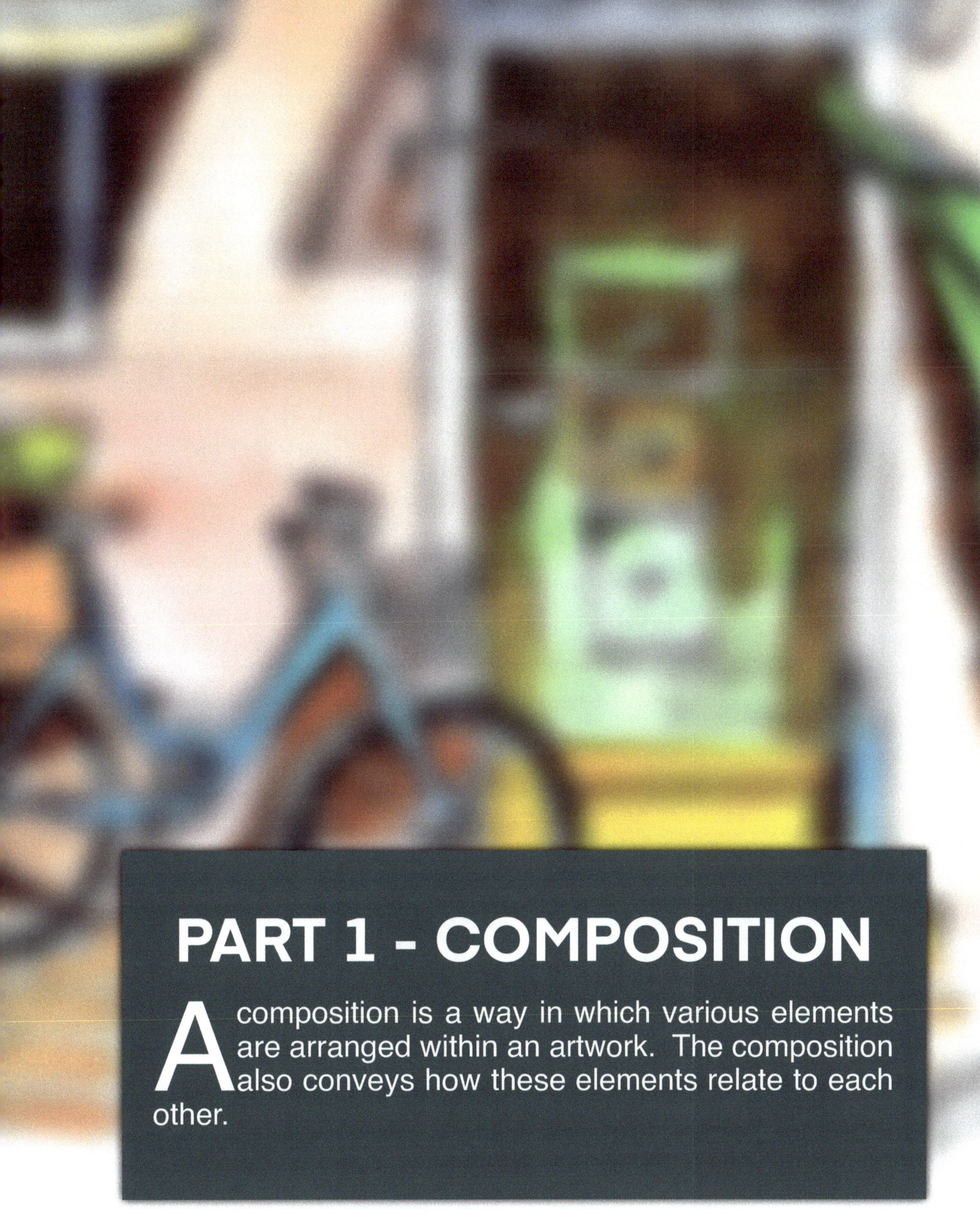

PART 1 - COMPOSITION

A composition is a way in which various elements are arranged within an artwork. The composition also conveys how these elements relate to each other.

Why Composition?

Have you ever visited a scenic spot bursting to the seams with the beauty of nature?

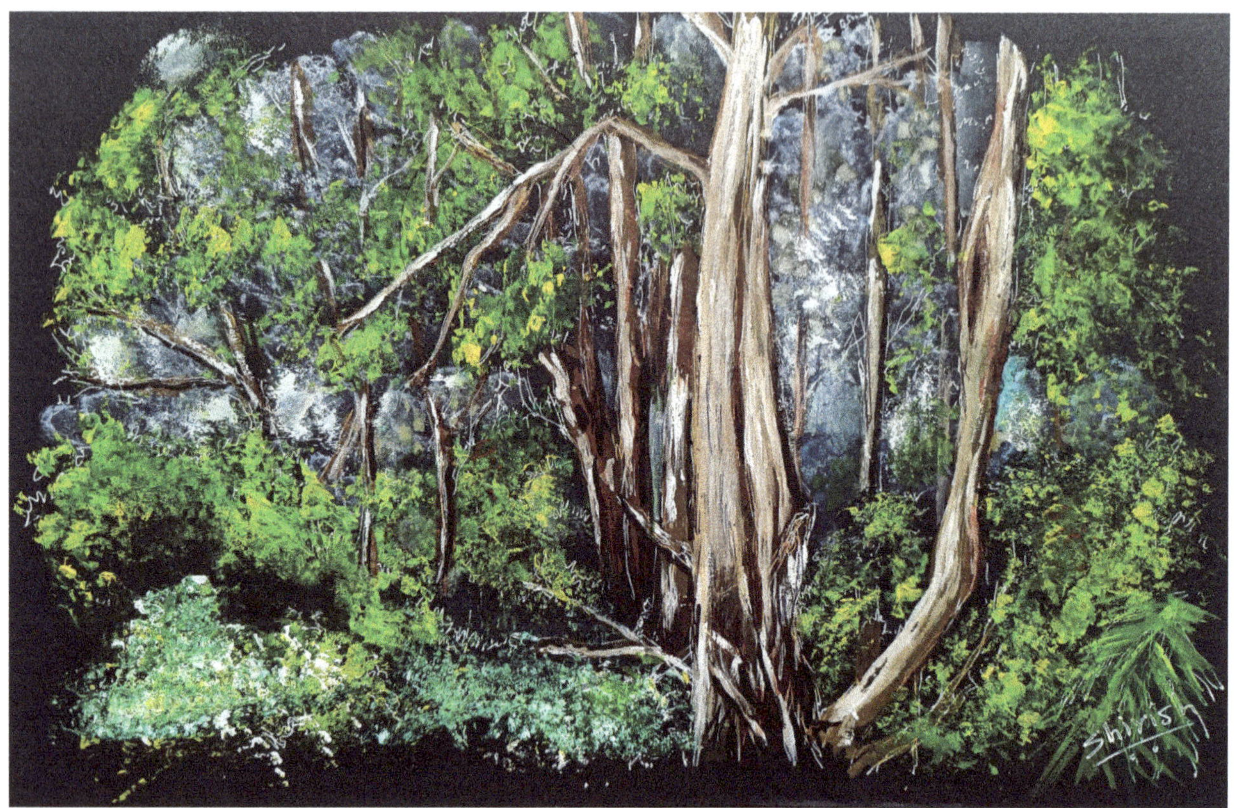

Did you feel compelled to click tons of photographs to preserve these memories?

And were you terribly disappointed when you viewed these photographs again?

Maybe because you could now see a pole jutting out of your partner's head!

Or you could now see that photobomber in the background. You had never noticed that when clicking the photograph!

And you are now thinking very hard. Why the hell did I not see that photobomber/pole/piece of garbage when I was clicking the picture?

There's a reason for it.

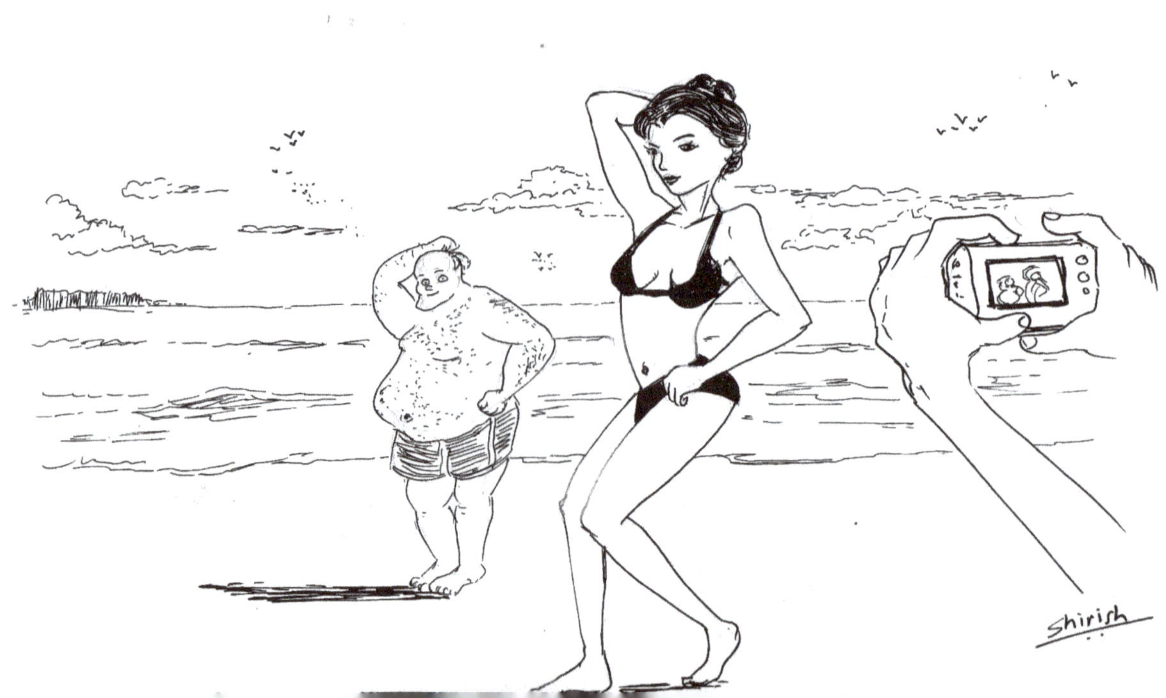

Sight and sound are our primary means to absorb the information the world is handing over to us.

And the world is handing over a lot of information to us!

Particularly in this era of constant social media distractions and information overload.

How many times did you check your phone in the last ten minutes?

You didn't?

Then most probably you have lost it, or the battery has died!

If we try to process every bit of information hurtling our way, we will be overwhelmed. Comatose. A vegetable. Our brain will have no time and energy to process everything and to do anything useful.

Thus, our brain applies a natural filter to the incoming information.

The brain lets in only that information which we think is relevant to us.

Now you know why you could hear everything but could not understand anything in that history class!

The same happens when we click that picture of our friend. We focus only on him/her, and not on what's behind them.

But the camera sees and records everything! There's no natural filter in the camera the way it's present in our brain.

On the other hand, some sketchers feel they should draw everything they see. They don't want to miss anything!

In fact, they believe in competing with the camera!

I feel pity for these poor souls. I really do.

Why?

Because they are squandering away a golden opportunity. The opportunity to pick and choose their composition. This freedom is seldom available to a photographer.

Being a sketcher, you have a power.

You have the power to select the elements you want in your sketch. You may choose their arrangement within the sketch. You may choose their juxtaposition.

Why waste this opportunity for the sake of plagiarizing reality?

As many a great people over the centuries have said... 'with great power comes great responsibility'.

I think Spiderman's uncle said the same thing, just before he died!

And as sketchers, our great responsibility is to be aware of the composition.

How?

Let's get to that now. But before we do, let's see how this book is arranged.

Composition and perspective are not independent elements. They complement each other within a picture.

In the first part of this book, we will learn some composition 'rules'. In the next part, we will learn about perspective.

While learning the perspective, I will point out the compositional elements that we learned in the first section. This will help you correlate them.

Ready to dive in? Let's begin!

'Rules' Of Composition

Before we dive into the rules of composition, let me clarify something.

Whenever I refer to a 'rule' about sketching, it's really a rule of thumb/guideline only.

As far as art is concerned, there are no rules! In fact, all the so-called rules in art are ripe for breaking.

The 'rules' that you will learn in this section are for you to make some conscious decisions for sketching.

Try to break these 'rules' and create more interesting compositions. I will be even happier if you do that.

So, let's get on with the 'rules'.

'Rule' #1: Balance (or the lack of it)

Have a look at the following picture. Do you see everything arranged so perfectly?

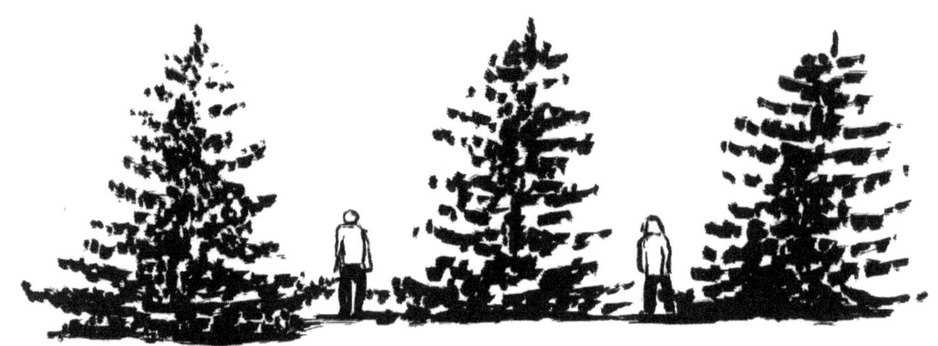

What does keeping everything so perfect and balanced inside the picture achieve? It makes the picture really dull, uninteresting and boring!

Why?

Because there's nothing for the viewer to imagine here.

Because the fun in art is all about imbalance!

We are subtly telling the viewer, 'I know you are absolutely dumb. So, I have made sure you see all I want to show you front and center! Don't look around. Don't imagine anything. Don't wander.'

How will you feel if someone tells you this?

Exactly!

That's why we need to bring in some degree of imbalance to the picture.

Look at the picture below. There's a little imbalance here. So it looks way more interesting than the earlier picture.

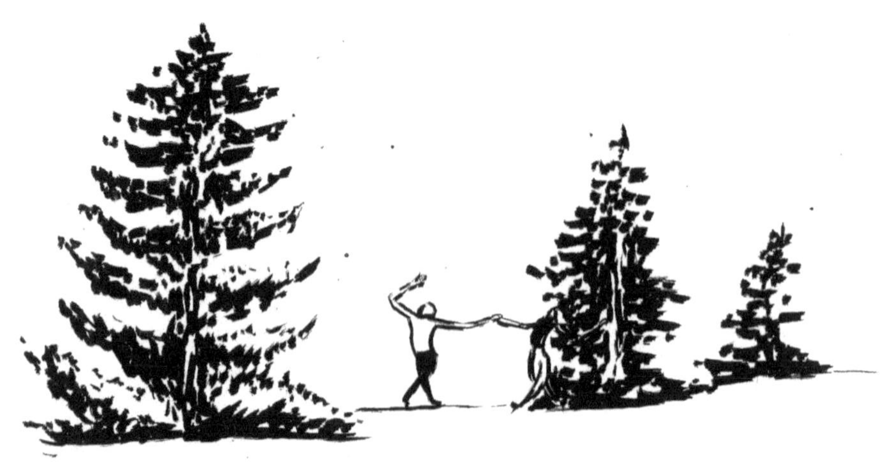

But if there's too much imbalance, the picture will be visually confusing.

If your goal is to make a picture visually confusing, go ahead and do it. Nothing wrong in it. But in most cases, we want to make our pictures clearer for the viewer's understanding.

That's why one needs to continually make a decision about this 'balance' factor in a sketch.

Fortunately, as a sketcher, we have the power to create this balance of elements as we see fit.

'Rule' #2: Rule of Thirds

Have a look at the following picture. Do you see the subject in the perfect center?

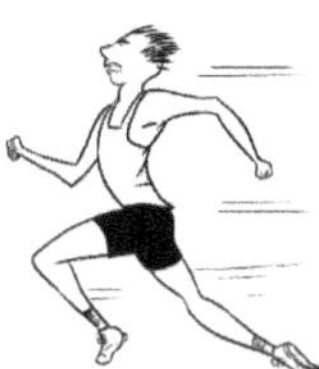

What's wrong with this picture?

Most of us will say … 'Nothing!'.

Why?

Because we are programmed to think that the main subject in a picture has to be at the center.

Well, here's a news flash.

keeping the subject in the exact center of the picture makes it really, really dull!

Why?

Because we are keeping it too much balanced (see 'rule' #1 above).

And, because everything is so centered, there's no dynamism to the picture.

Let me explain what I mean.

Have a look at this picture below.

When you see this picture, what do you see?

Do you see *just* a runner?

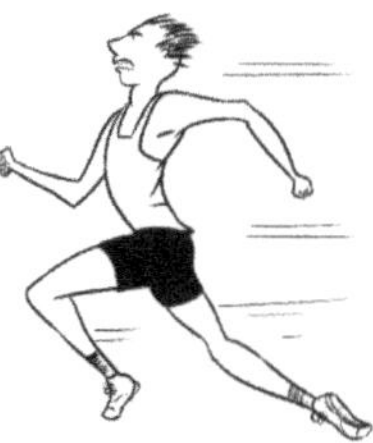

Or do you see *possibilities*?

When you place the subject on one side of the frame, what happens?

The viewer will not only see the main subject but mentally fills in the details.

In this case, you are respecting the intelligence of the viewer. The viewer subtly understands this.

It also keeps the possibilities of seeing more than what is being shown.

If you think the above paragraph is too philosophical... It's time to take a deep breath and not go away just yet.

Because I will now explain the same stuff in plain language and pictures!

Let's have a look at some pictures and see how the 'rule' of the third is in effect, starting with the above example:

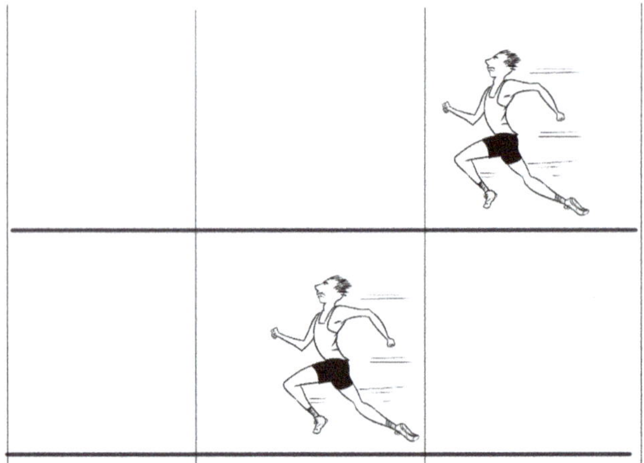 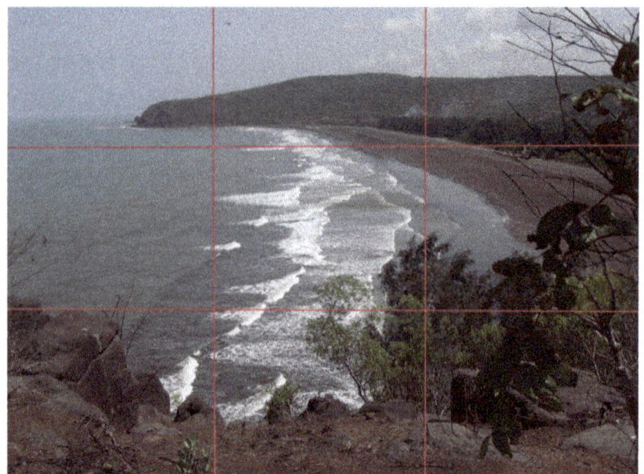

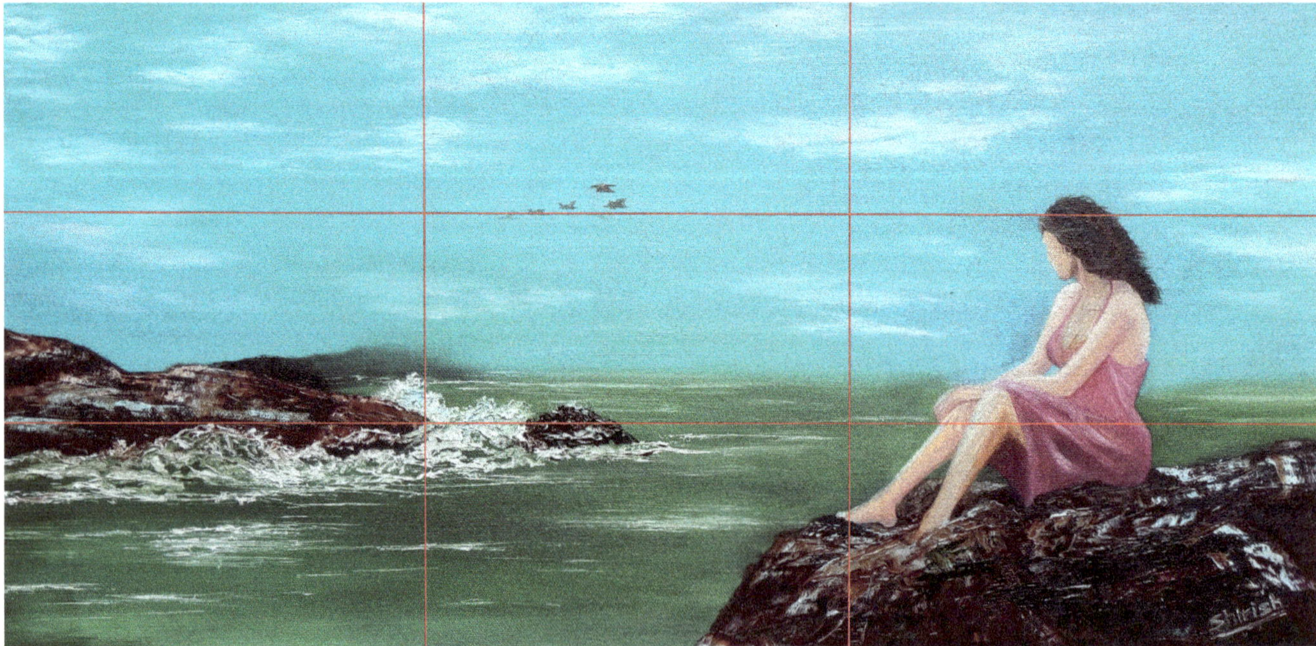

But I repeatedly stress this all the time.

There are no concrete rules in the realm of arts. And all the so-called rules are meant to be broken.

So, here's one example where the 'rule' of thirds is broken. Observe how the main subject is smack in the middle of the picture. The picture is divided into two equal halves (upper half and lower half).

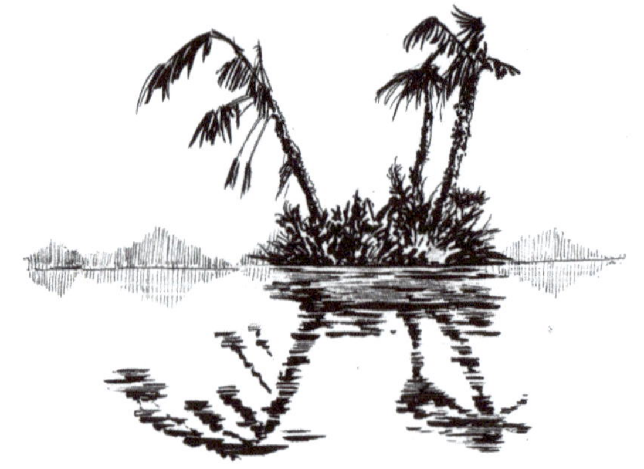

    Composition and Perspective

'Rule' #3: Overlapping

If we are looking at doing realist drawings, we typically place several elements in a picture.

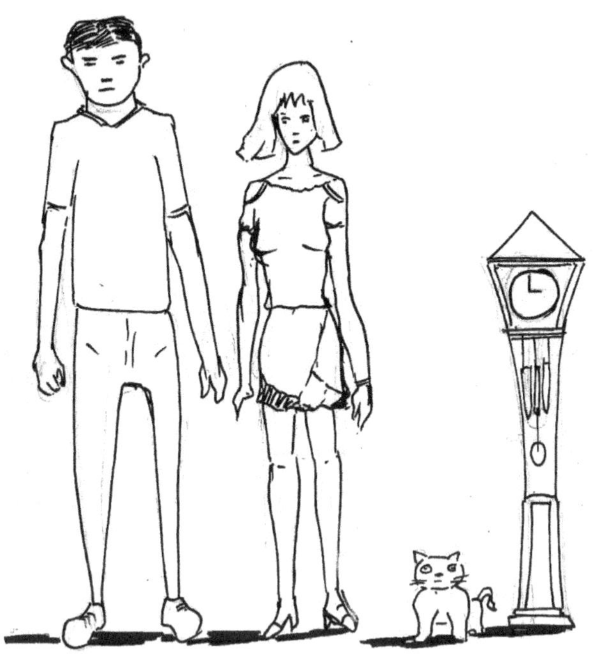

When the viewer sees a picture, he/she is not merely observing each element individually. They also sense the relationships between these elements.

Have a look at this picture. Do you feel something is amiss here (except that this picture is really… really crude)?

You may not be able to tell consciously what's wrong with this picture, because technically, there's nothing wrong here (except that it's really… really crude!).

But still, it feels odd because no two elements in this picture are overlapping.

To lend some believability to the picture, it's necessary that at least some elements overlap.

Why is this even needed?

Look at it this way.

We are sketching a 3D scene over a flat (2D) paper.

To create an illusion of a 3D scene on this flat paper, we need to arrange our composition in a certain way. It must make the viewer's mind think that there's depth to the scene.

Overlapping is a perfect way to create this illusion.

Yet, for most artists, overlapping is a thorn which they would rather avoid.

Why?

Because overlapping demands certain planning on the part of the artist.

And most artists think that art is a completely spontaneous process. If one introduces an element of planning in it, the art will lose its magic.

Nothing can be further from the truth.

Art can be planned and still preserve its spontaneity and the X-factor.

Here's an example of a picture where there's ample overlap to create the illusion of depth.

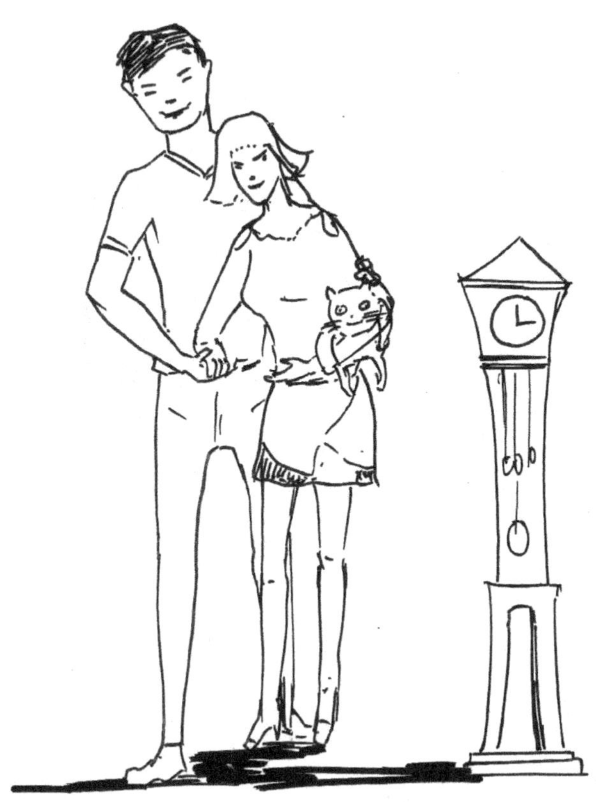

Rule' #4: Foreground, middleground, and background

Since we are talking about depth and overlap, it's important to talk about foreground, middleground and background.

The picture can be divided into three virtual layers.

a) Foreground - The elements closest to the viewer.

b) Background - The farthest part from the viewer.

c) Middleground - The elements between foreground and background.

All these layers compliment and contrast each other to create depth in the picture.

It's up to the artist which layer should have more emphasis.

Below, the picture on the left is an example of a picture where the emphasis is on the foreground. The middle picture is an example of the same picture where the emphasis is on the middleground. The right-hand side picture is an example of the same picture where the emphasis is on the background.

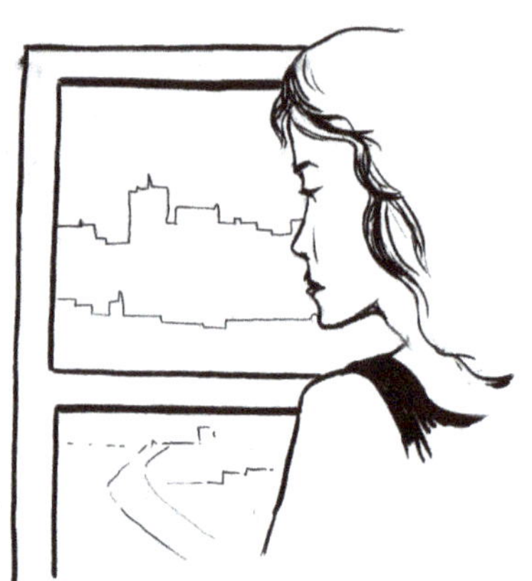 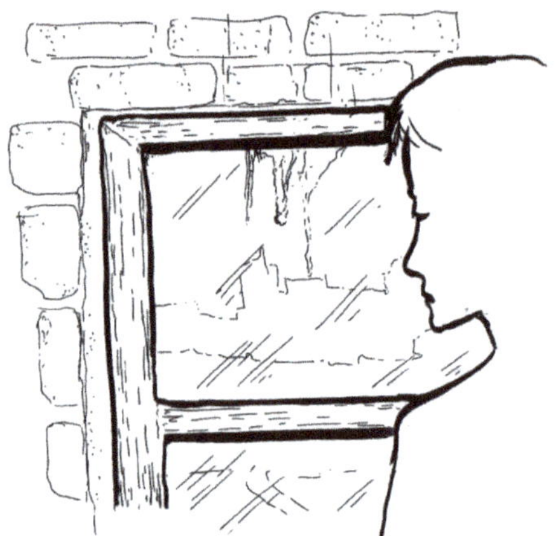 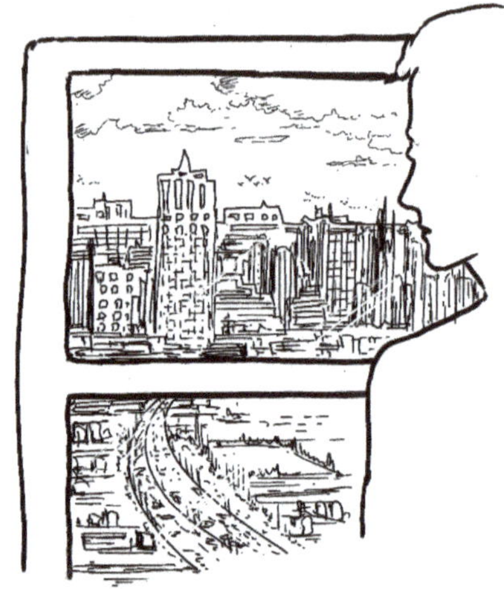

In fact, there's no need to keep all three 'grounds' in the picture.

Some pictures can have the only foreground and background layers, and no middleground.

See the picture of an abandoned car below. The main subject (the car) is in the foreground, while everything else is in the background.

But you may argue that the tree on the right is in the middleground. It's closer to the viewer than the mountains behind.

Valid point. But I have treated is as background!

This argument proves one more point.

Foreground, middleground and background are relative notions envisioned by the artist. It's up to you to decide which is which and proceed with your own judgment.

Hence, it's proven that this particular picture has only a foreground and a background!

Let's move ahead.

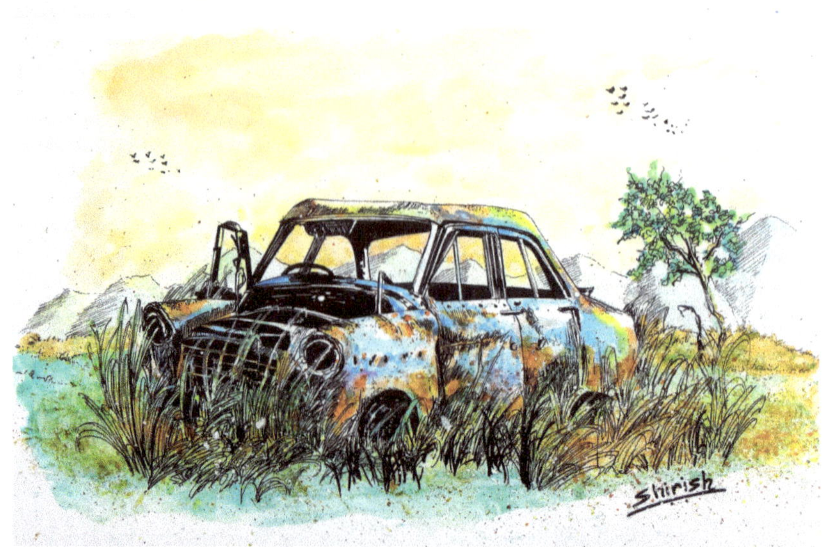

Rule' #5: Frame within frame

This 'rule' builds over the 'rule #4' discussed just now, and the 'rule' of overlapping discussed before.

In this rule, we use a foreground element as a 'frame' for the background.

The foreground frame is almost always de-emphasized.

Bonus: Want to see how this picture was sketched? Head over to this URL:

https://youtu.be/5JKf2rFzsJc

Alternatively, use the QR code given below to watch the complete video of the making of this sketch. And don't forget to subscribe to the channel!

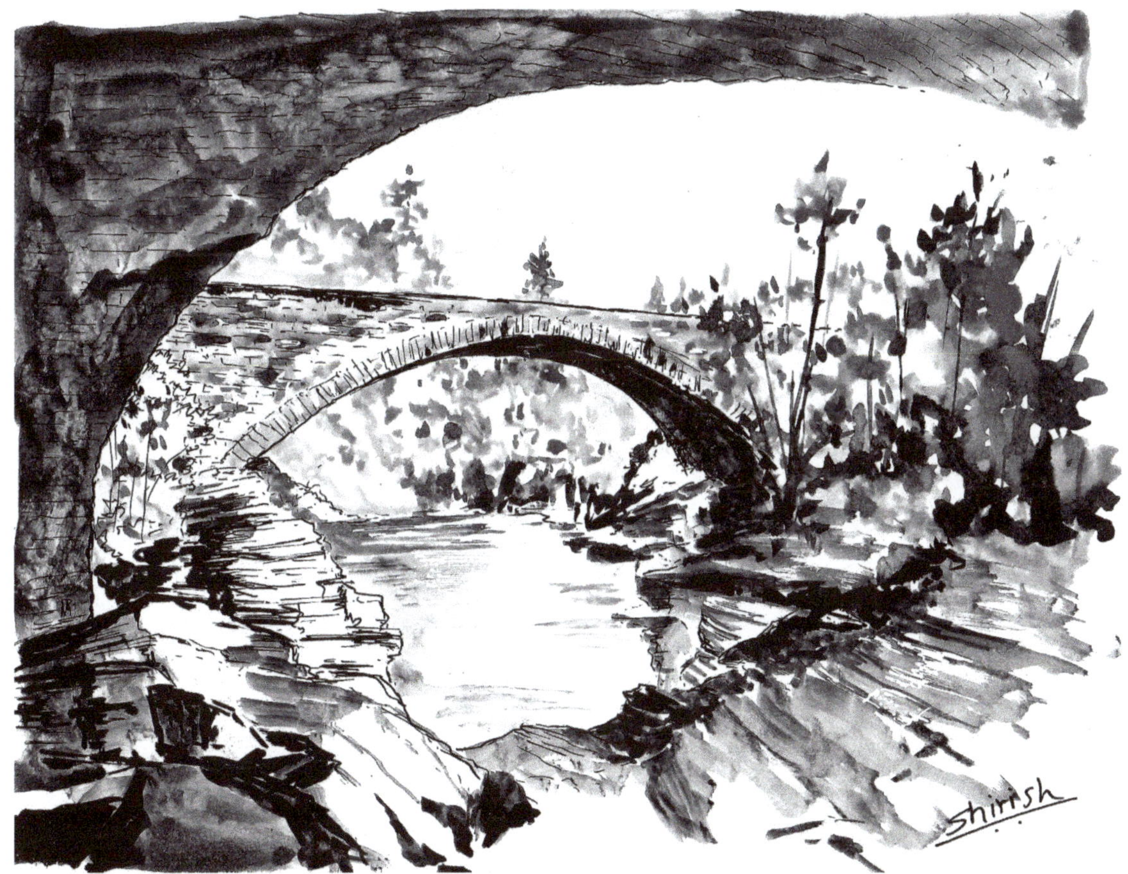

What effect does using a foreground element as a frame have?

It automatically pushes the other elements back, creating depth in the picture.

But again, what's the point of having a rule if we cannot break it?

Remember what I said on the previous page?

The foreground frame is almost always de-emphasized.

Let's break this 'rule' now.

In the picture on the next page, the foreground 'frame' is the central element. All other elements visible through the frame are de-emphasized.

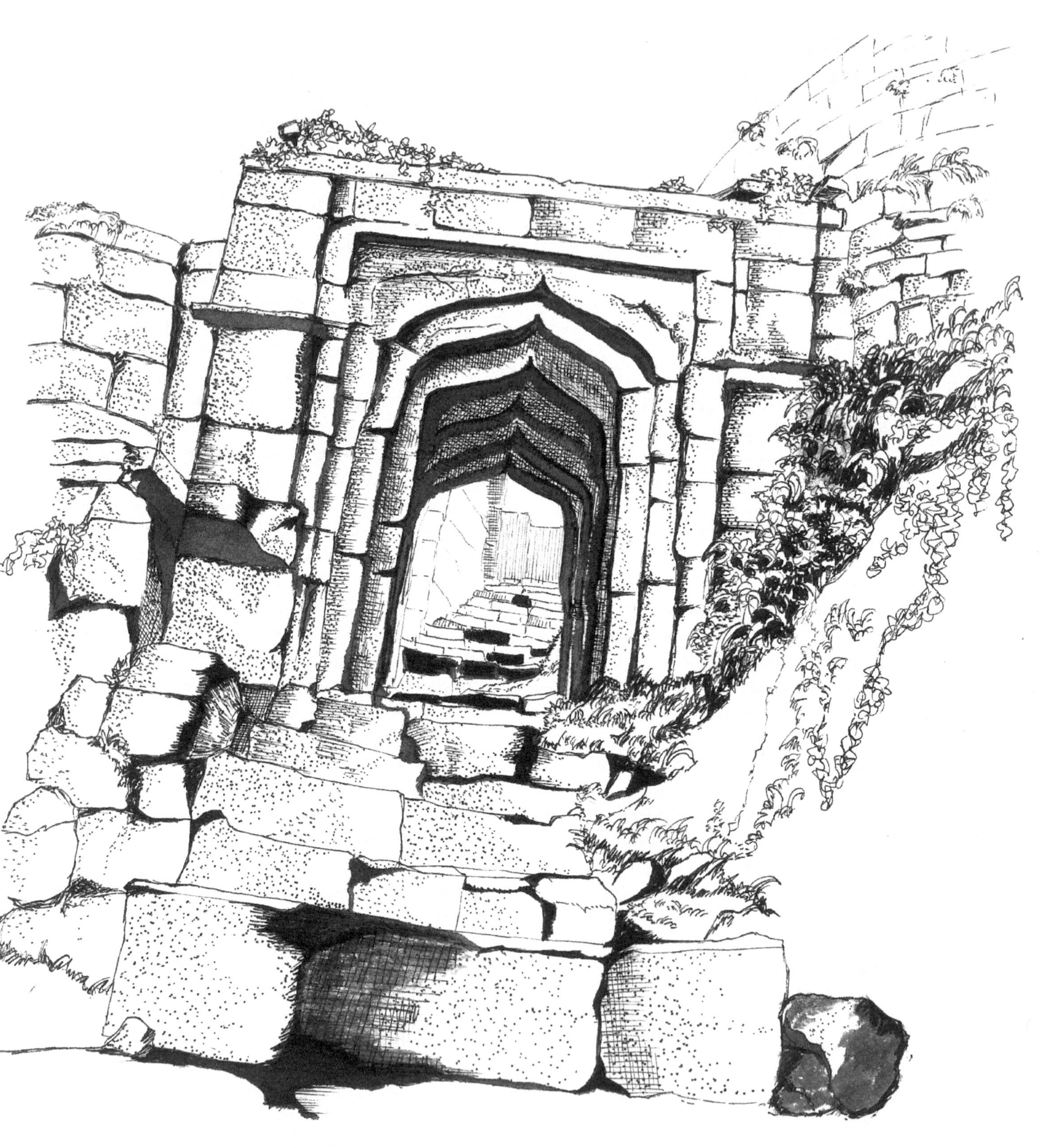

Composition and Perspective

'Rule' #6: Leading the viewer's eye

This 'rule' is the culmination of all the previous 'rules'.

*   Balance

*   Rule of thirds

*   Overlapping

*   Layers like foreground, middleground, and background

*   Frame within a frame.

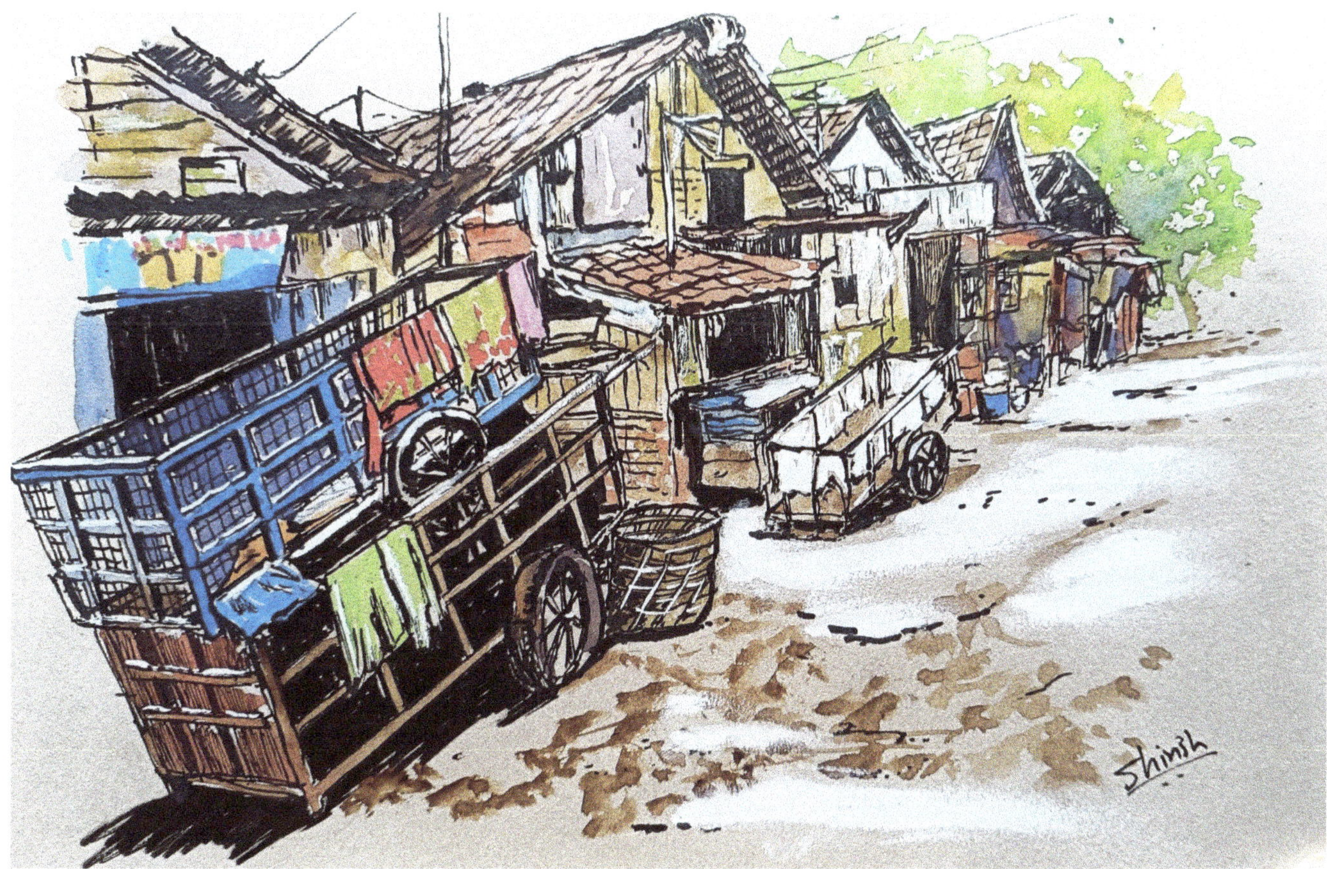

This 'rule' is not so much about one aspect of the composition. But it's about the overall impact of a composition on the viewer's mind.

You see, how a viewer's eye wanders over your creation is the key to how it will influence him/her.

Give the viewer more opportunities to discover different elements in your picture. The viewer will fall in love with your artwork.

And the way to influence this is to decide how you want the eye of the viewer to wander inside your picture.

Before this stuff becomes too heavy, let's see this with an example.

In the picture above, the road leads the eye from the bottom left towards the horizon. The viewer feels that he/she is actually entering the picture.

You may use various tricks to lead the eye into the picture as follows. These are some of the tricks that I use, or I have seen other artists use. But don't keep yourself limited to those. You can always invent new stuff as an artist!

a) Keep your main subject on the right side of the picture using 'rule' of the third - Most of the people in the world write from left to right (with some exceptions like Arabic script). So people tend to 'read' the picture from left to right.

If you keep the main subject to the left side of the picture, the viewer may lose interest quickly. This is because they have already seen what's important in the picture.

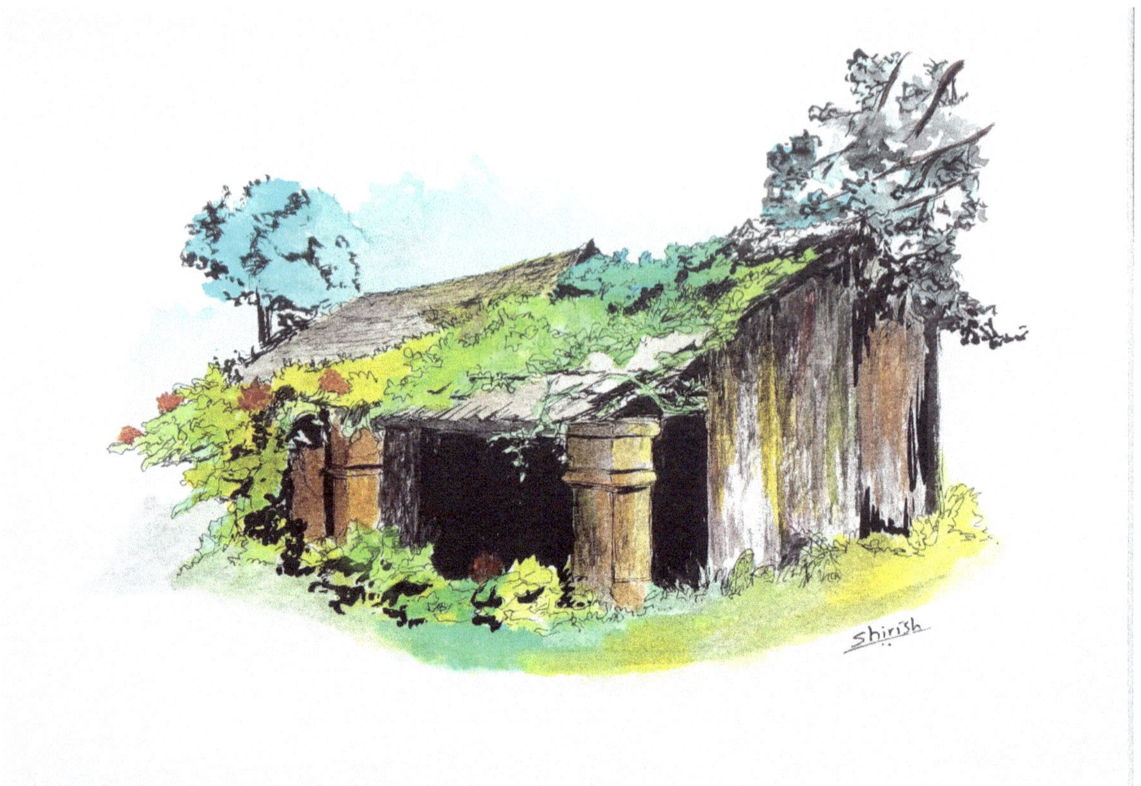

b) Using lines at an angle (next page) - This comes in handy while sketching/painting certain elements like:

- Roads

- Rivers

- Railroads

- Benches

- Any other elements with parallel edges

If you draw such elements horizontally, they may look boring (too much balance). But if you draw them at an angle, the viewer's eye will follow the lines 'inside' the sketch/painting.

c) Using frame within a frame - This automatically creates a 'window' effect for the viewer. Try further using the middle/background elements to draw the viewer's eye inside the picture. It will create a pleasing composition.

This is already discussed at length in 'rule' #5 above.

d) Overlapping can be used to lead the viewer's eye inside the picture. When the viewer sees a picture, what does his/her eye automatically see? Of course the foreground elements.

The viewer's eye will follow the lines leading from the foreground elements towards the background elements.

Refer the first picture of the village in this 'rule' to see what I mean.

In fact, all the so-called 'rules' we discussed are not independent of each other. They all compliment and build over each other. I broke them down as separate 'rules' only for our easy understanding.

And don't forget the most important fact. Each one of these 'rules' is meant to be broken. So don't be too rigid about these 'rules'. They are only guidelines, not something set in stone.

With that one more philosophical dialogue, we will move to the next compositional 'rule'.

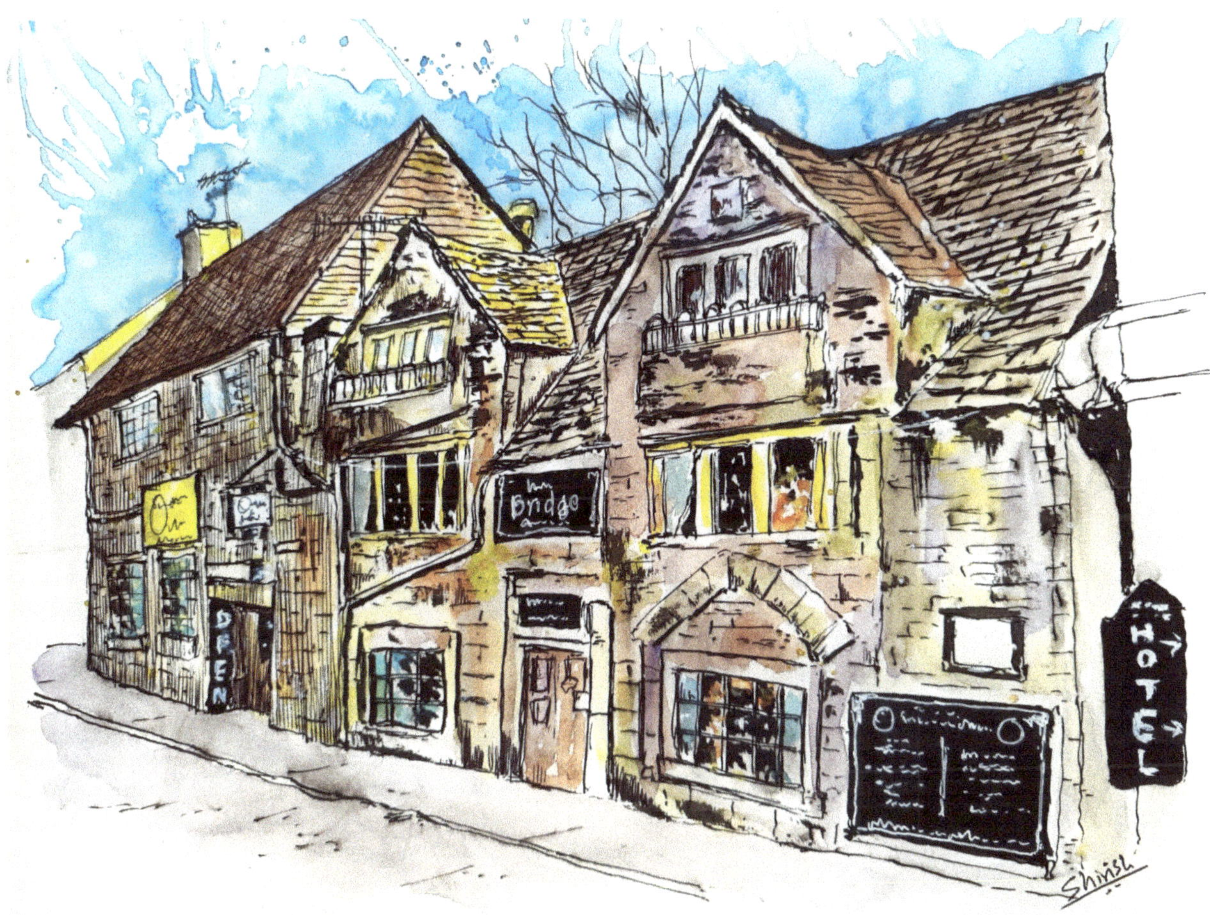

Bonus: Want to see how this picture was sketched? Head over to the URL given below to watch the complete video of the making of this sketch. And don't forget to subscribe to the channel!

https://youtu.be/aIQ4stgycNk?si=fP33twklzkp47vj9

Alternatively, use the QR code given below to watch the complete video of the making of this sketch. And don't forget to subscribe to the channel!

'Rule' #7: 'Sizing' the elements

This 'rule' is about influencing the size of an element in the viewer's mind using the way it's depicted in a picture.

Recall a fantasy movie you have seen.

When a giant monster enters the scene, where's the camera placed?

Always at the foot of the monster, looking up.

When an element is seen from its bottom, looking up, it feels large in size (refer to the picture on the next page to see what I mean).

But when one is looking at an element from the top, the element looks smaller and even insignificant.

This is a frequent travesty committed when clicking children's photographs.

When photographing a child, or any person, always get to their level. It creates much better, flattering images.

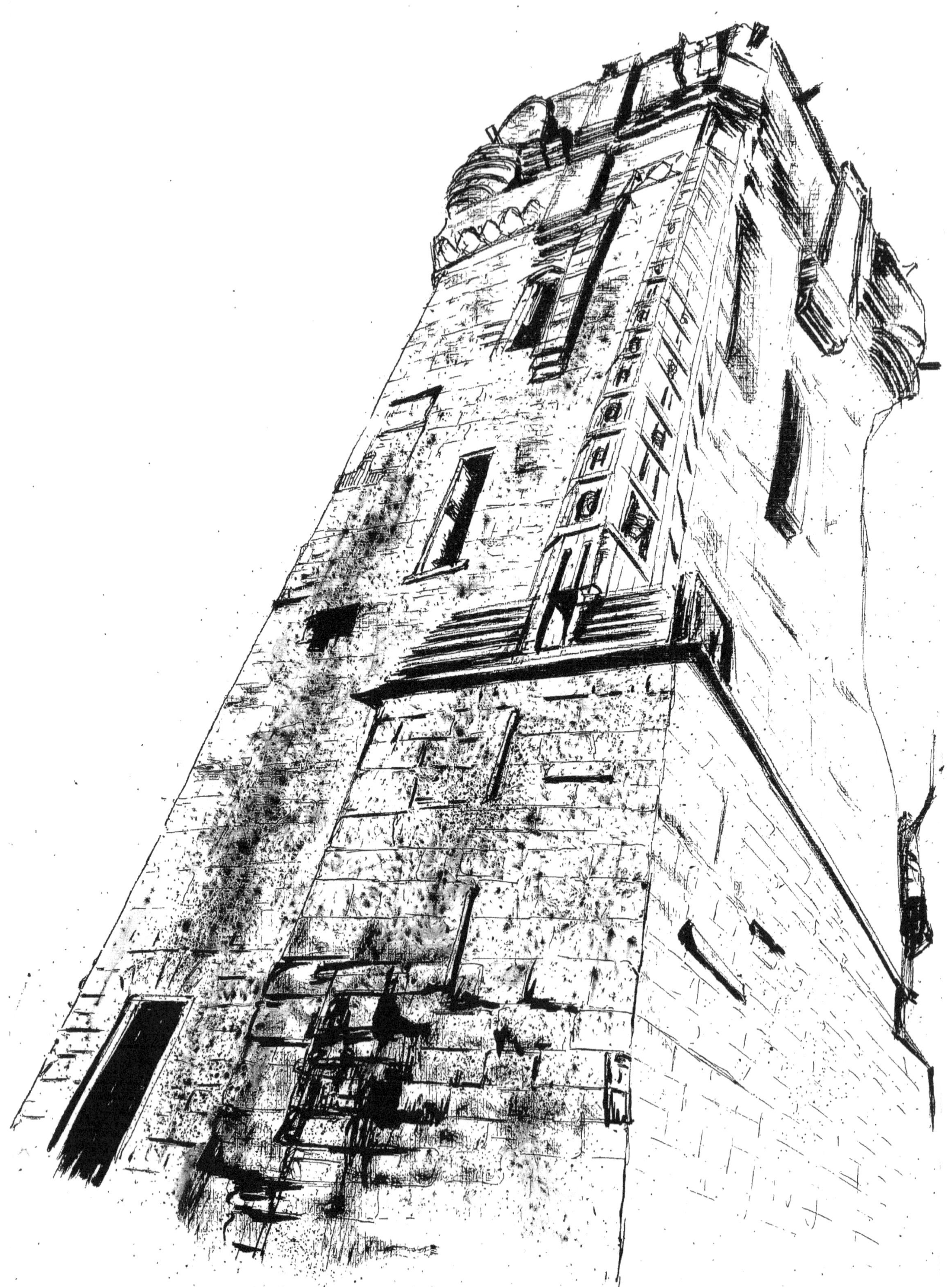

'Rule' #8: Emphasizing and de-emphasizing elements (visual weight)

This 'rule' builds over all the 'rules' mentioned earlier.

The whole point of planning the composition is to influence the viewer. We want the viewer to see our creation in a certain way. We want to emphasize and de-emphasize the elements within our picture to control this experience.

By default, all the elements within a picture are equal.

But to make things more interesting, some elements within the picture may be made 'more equal'!

Have a look at the picture below on the left. Everything is shown at the same level of emphasis.

Below right is the same picture where some of the elements are emphasized. You can see right away how much less cluttered this image looks.

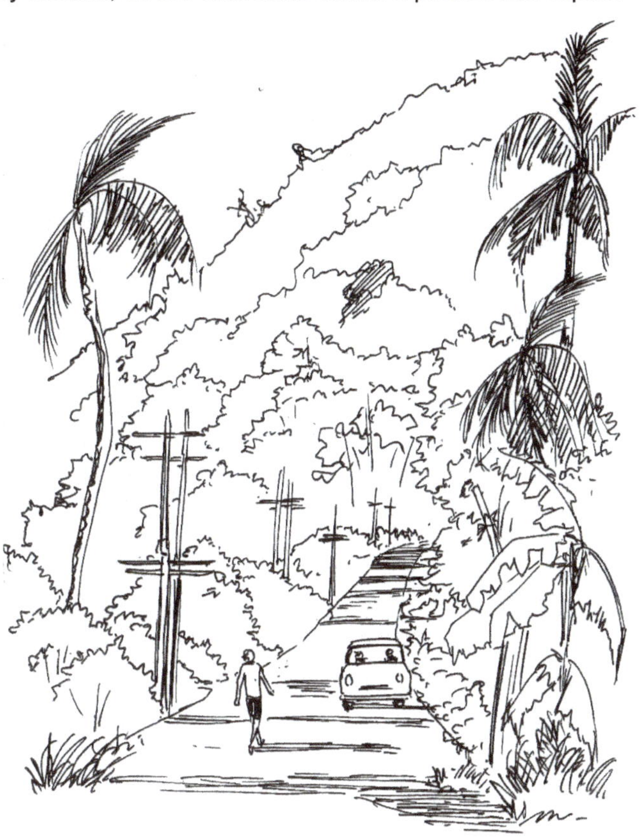

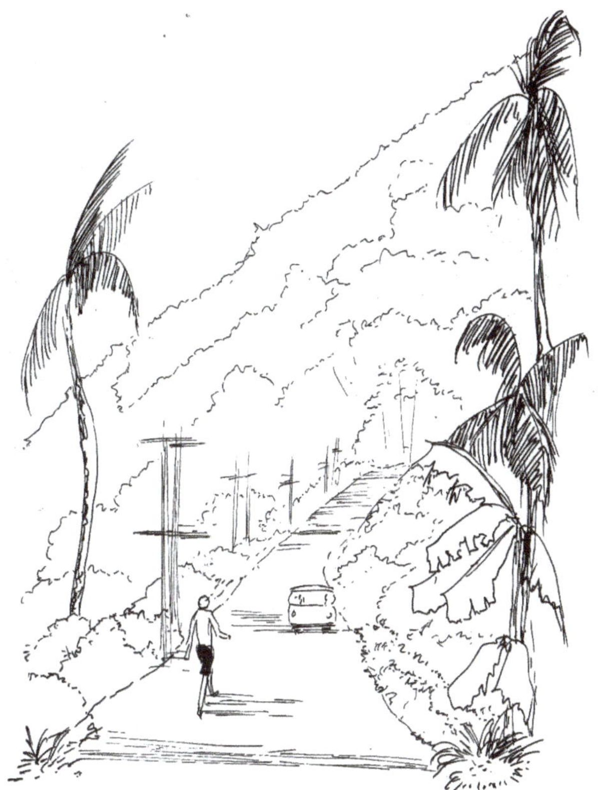

You may control emphasis on elements using various methods. Following are some methods frequently employed.

This is in no way a comprehensive list, and many more methods are being invented even as I write it.

*   Use thicker lines to outline the elements of emphasis. Use thinner lines for others (This is done in the example we just discussed above).

*   Show more details in the elements of importance and reduce details in the others. See the picture on the right for an example.

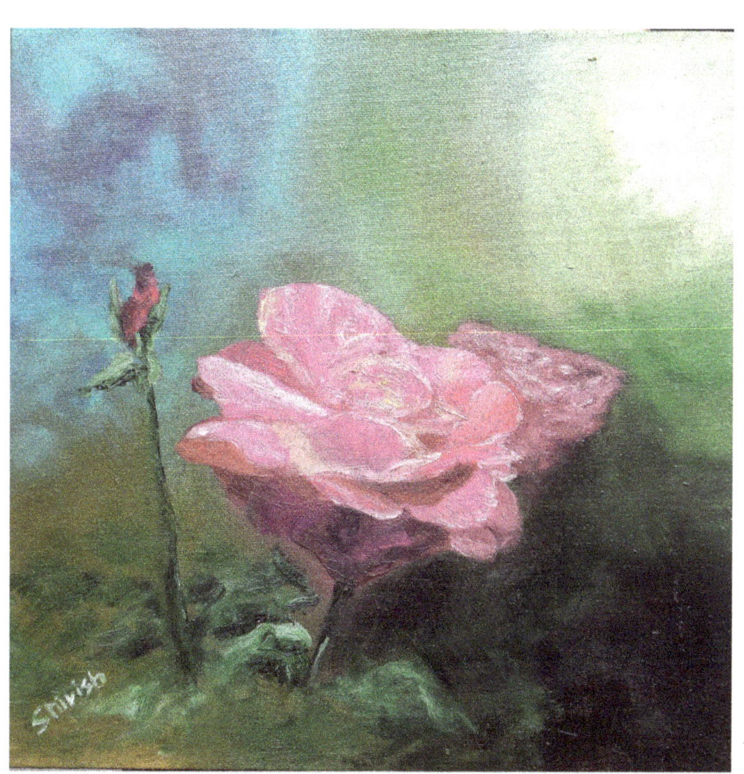

- Use wider aperture setting while photographing to blur the background. An equivalent effect can be achieved in a painting as well. See the example below.

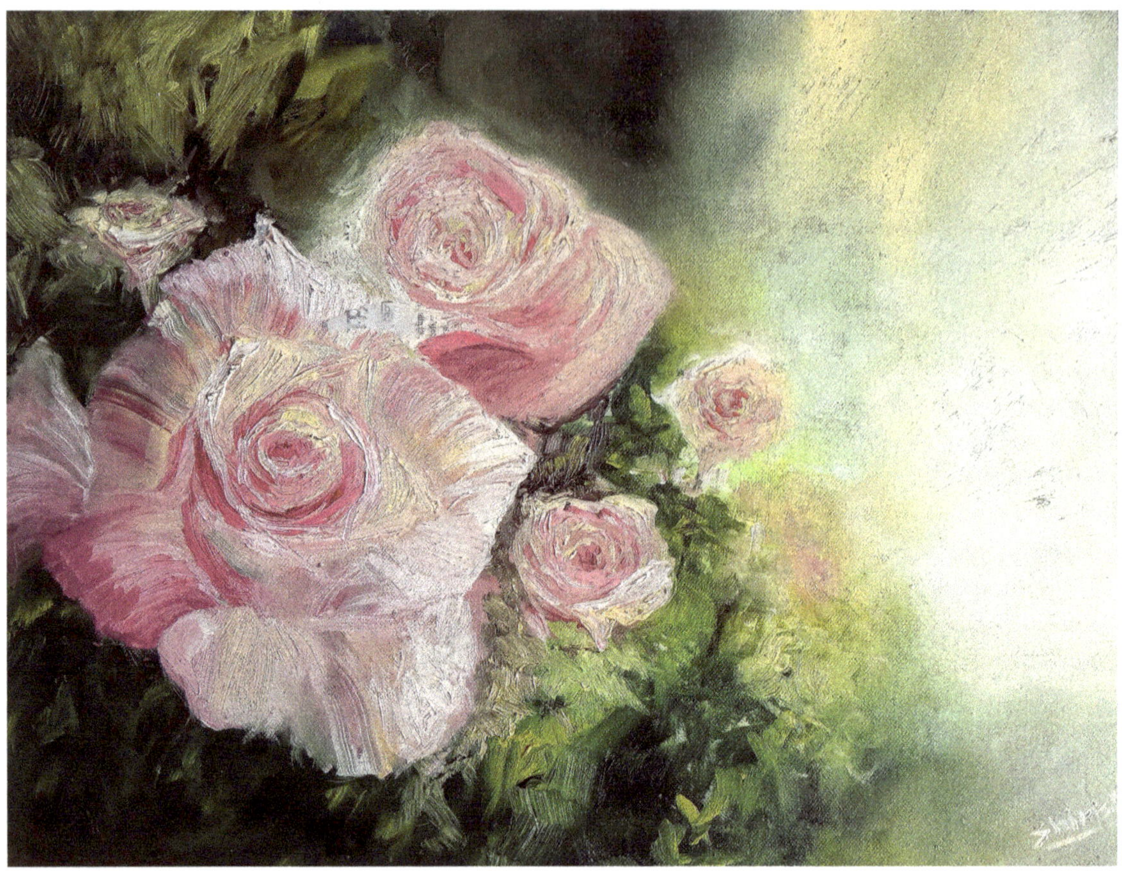

- Use borderless outlines/silhouettes to push elements in the background. See the picture below for example.

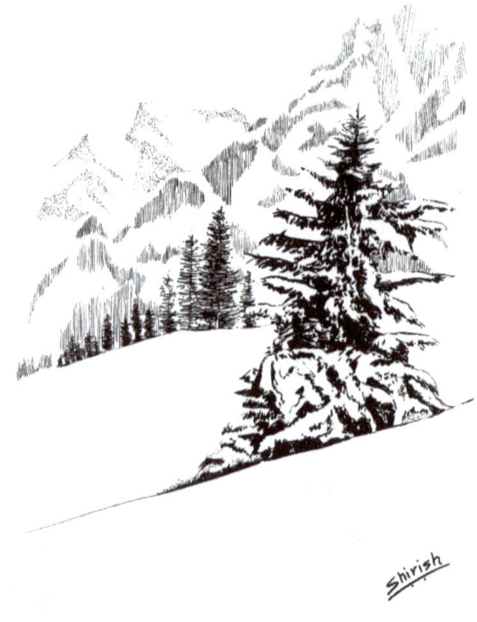

Composition and Perspective

- Use brighter colors for elements of emphasis and more greys/muted colors for others. See this example. Here, the coffee cup and the water droplets over the window pane are highlighted. The rest of the picture is practically grey.

Is it mandatory to highlight some elements like this? Absolutely not! Sometimes, you may want to have all elements having the same level of importance in your picture. There are no concrete rules as far as art is concerned.

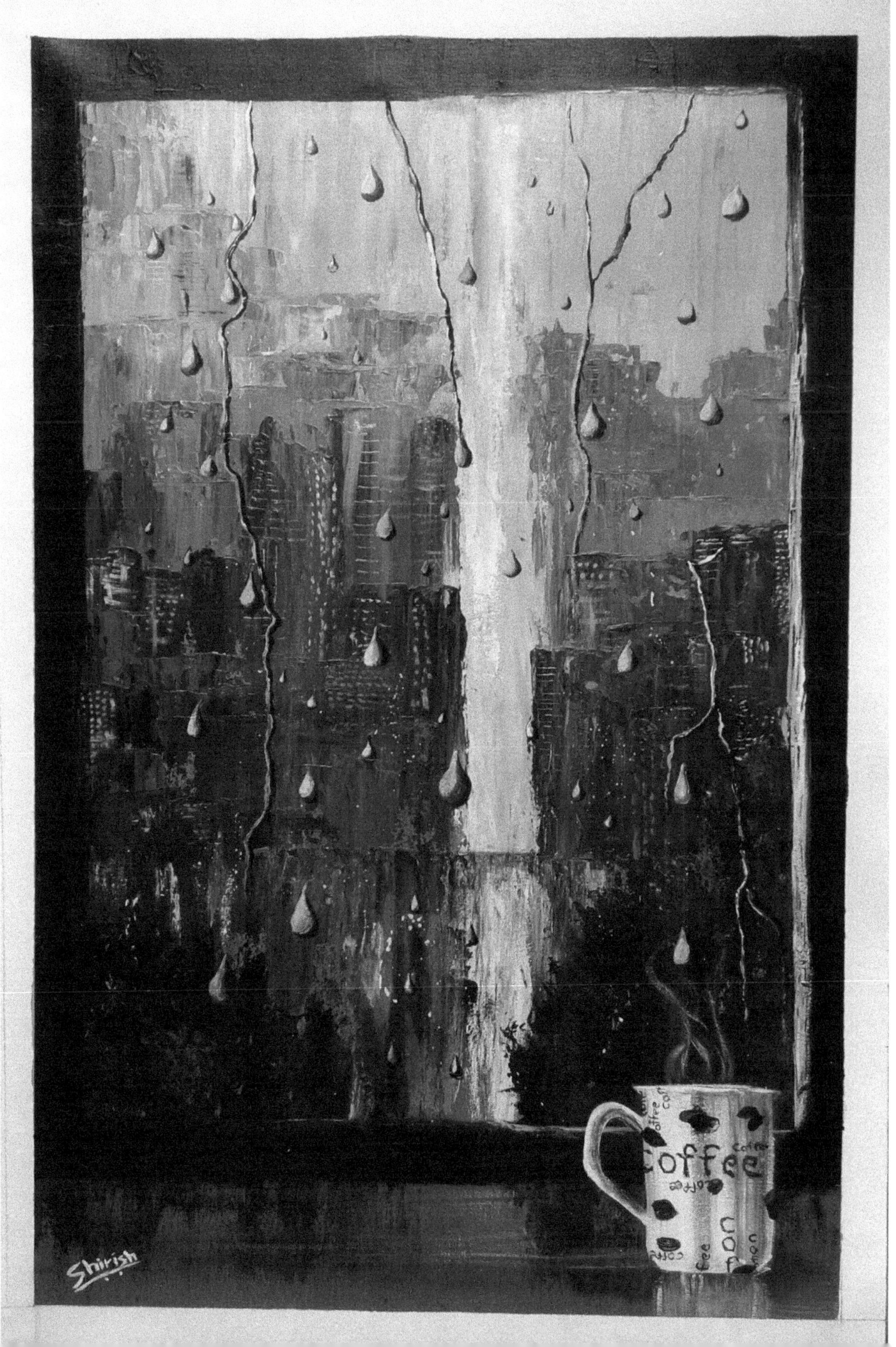

'Rule' #9: Using white space/negative space/empty space

There's a very popular delusion many artists live by.

Every nook and cranny of the paper/canvas needs to be filled up.

Nothing can be further from the truth.

In fact, the negative space in a sketch/painting can greatly improve the effectiveness of the picture.

How so?

The white space provides a much needed 'breathing space' for the elements.

(See the 'rule' #1 for balancing the elements).

The white space can act as an important element to stimulate possibilities in the viewer's mind. (see the 'rule' #2 for example in 'rule of thirds').

The white space can be used to lead the viewer's eye within the picture (see 'rule' #6).

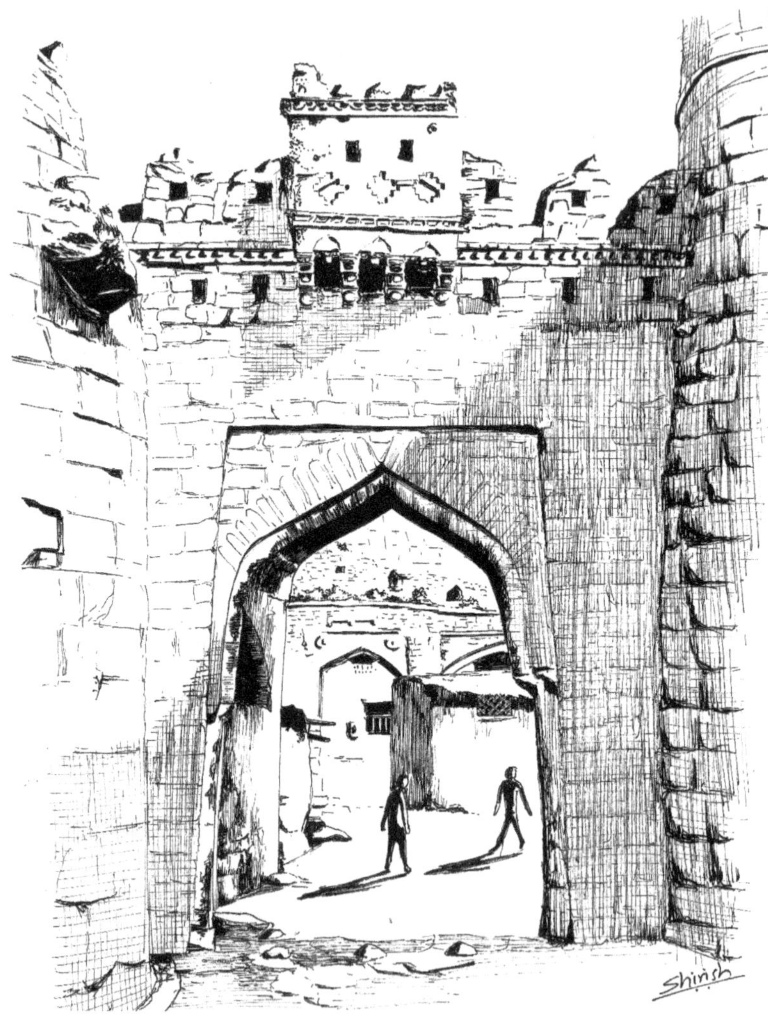

Do you see a pattern here?

Can you see that I am referring to the 'rules' already explained for explaining the new 'rules'?

Is it laziness?

Maybe!

But there's more than laziness at work here.

All these 'rules' are intertwined, and they cannot be separated from each other.

They are explained as separate 'rules' just to simplify them for understanding.

The picture above is an example of white spaces being used effectively to add to the beauty of a picture. You can see the bright light effect created by white spaces and dark areas around those spaces.

An example of all the 'rules' working together

I will say that again which I have repeatedly stressed throughout this section.

All the so-called 'rules' of the composition are intertwined. They should not be looked at independent from each other.

Let's look at this picture again and see how it measures up to those 'rules'.

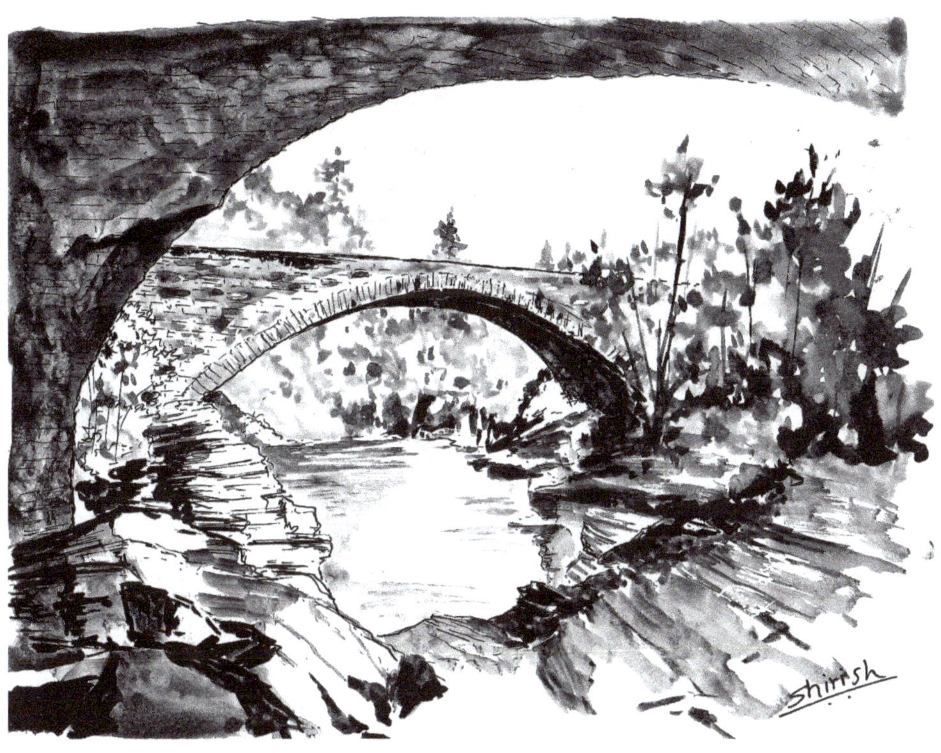

1. Balance: Observe how the elements in this picture are just out of balance. Observe how the different shapes are juxtaposed. This is done without creating clutter. The picture appears to somewhat tilt towards the left, creating an interest. Also, observe that no arrow is perfectly horizontal/vertical.

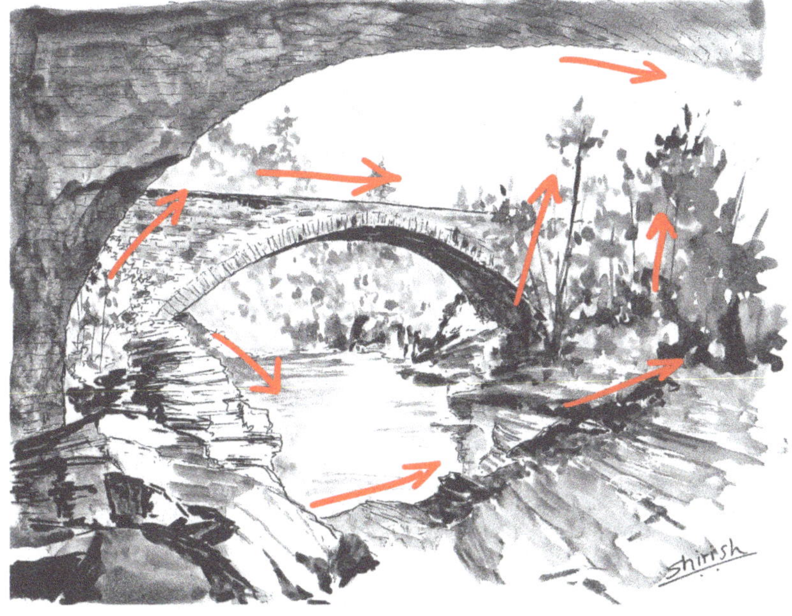

2. Rule of Thirds: The division shown here is self-explanatory enough!

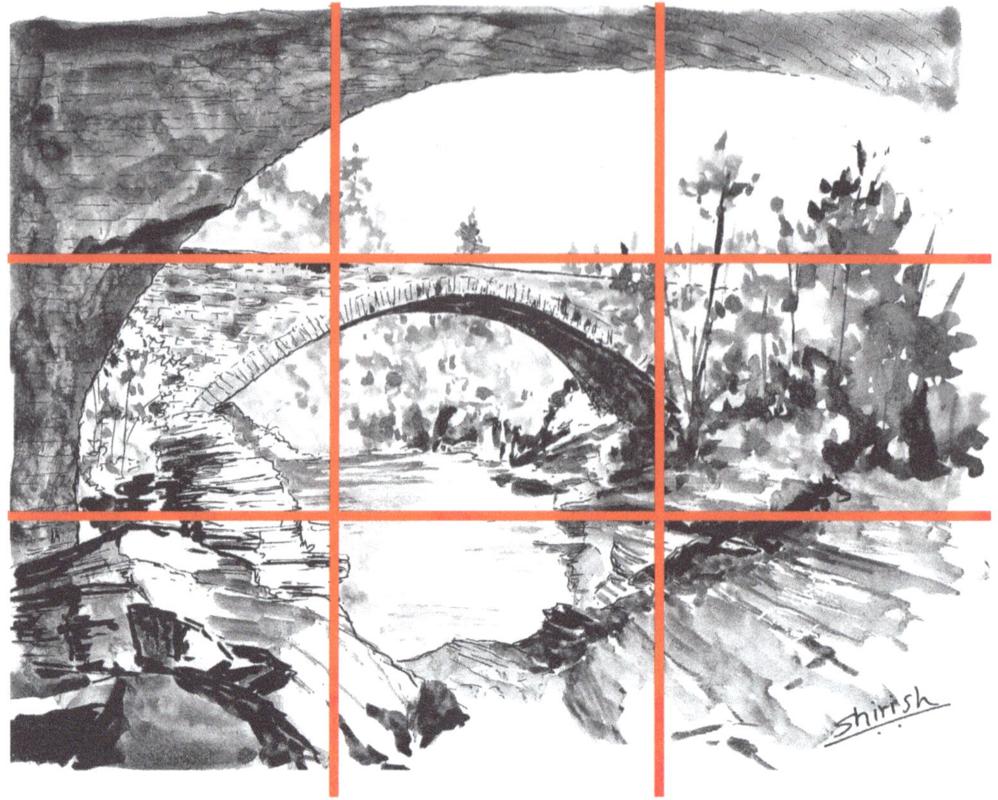

3. Overlapping: Observe how the various elements overlap.

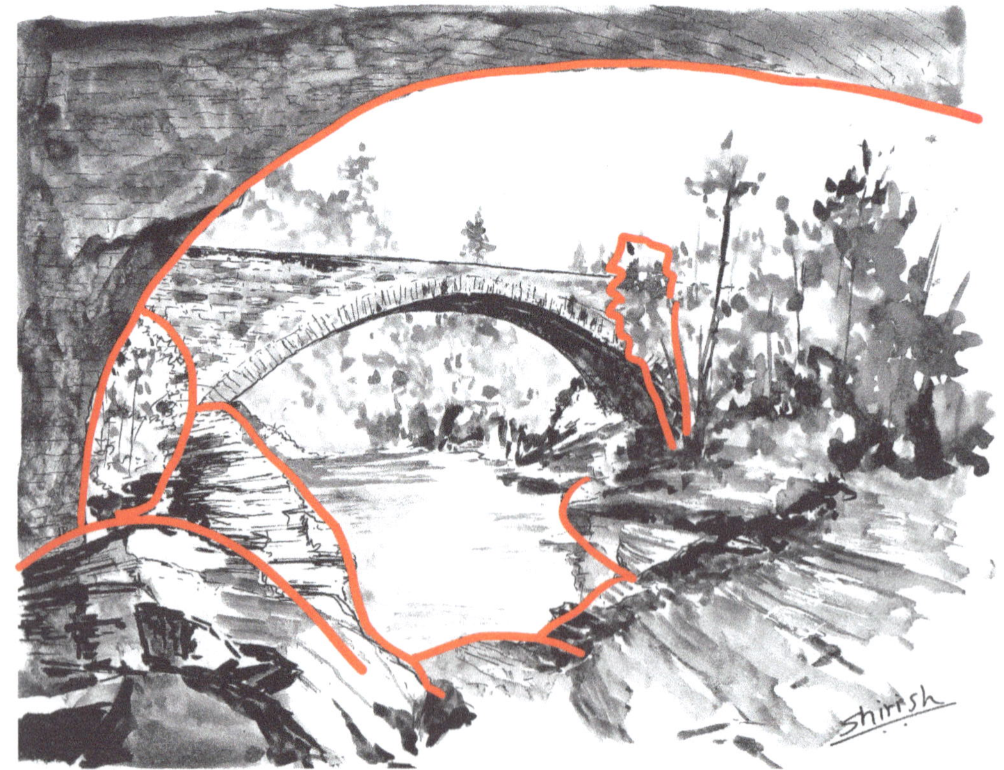

4. Foreground, Middleground, and Background: See how the various elements in this picture are distinctly placed at three levels of depth.

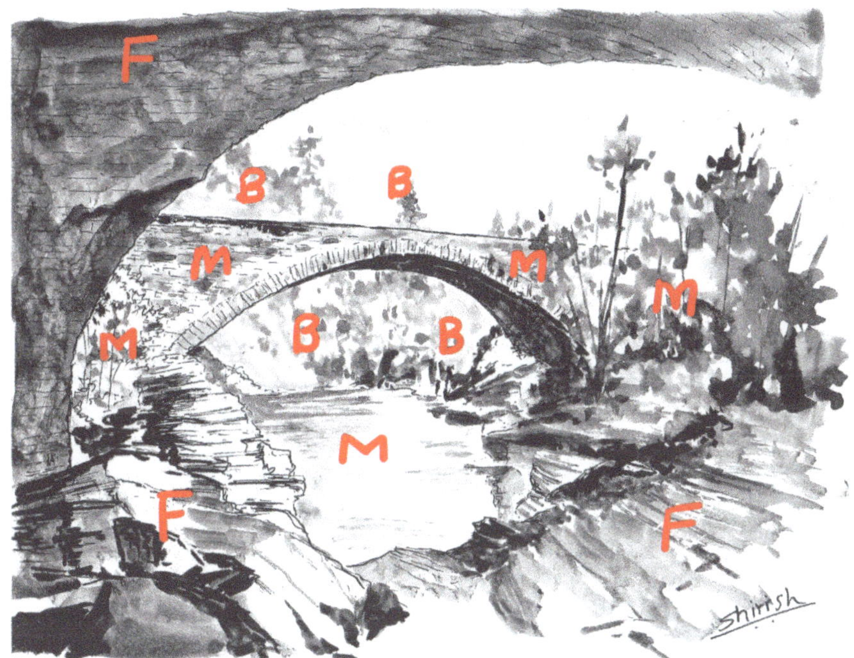

5. Frame within the frame: This has already been discussed about this picture. No need to repeat it!

6. Leading the viewer's eye: Starting with 'S' in the picture below, the viewer's eye traces the picture as per the arrows are shown.

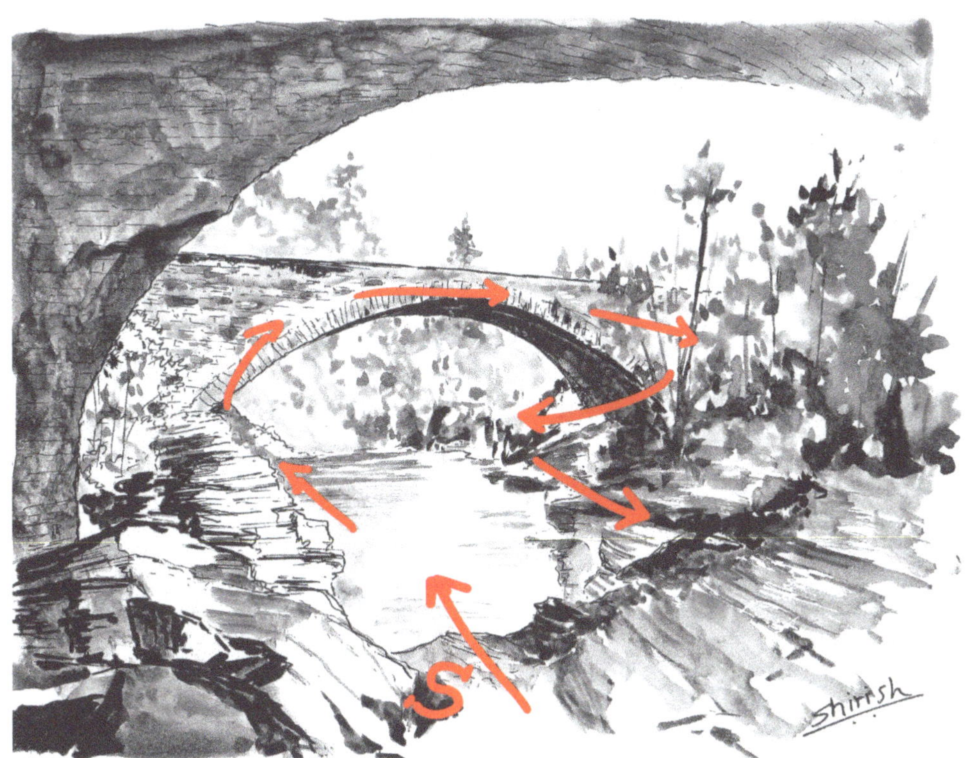

7. 'Sizing' the elements: In this picture, we are not looking at any element from above or below. But there's a different trick used to indicate their size. The stone bridge is juxtaposed against the tall trees to indicate its size. We have also made use of the horizon (our eye level) here. We will learn more about the horizon in the Perspective section.

The elements placed above the horizon line appear big, and vice versa.

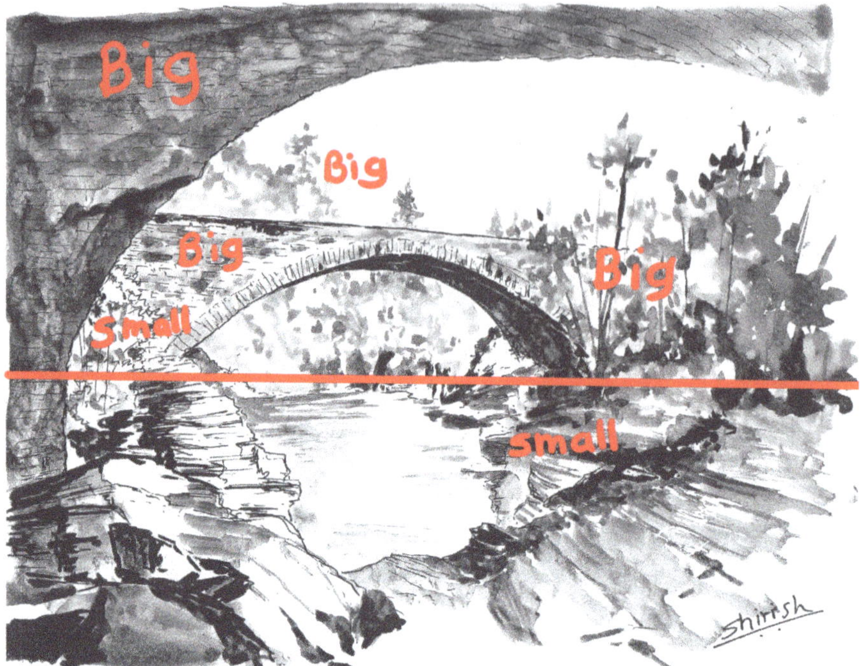

8. Emphasizing and De-emphasizing elements (Visual Weight): The emphasized elements are denoted by 'E'. The de-emphasized elements are indicated by 'D'. The closest element (the big foreground arch) is de-emphasized. This is done by showing it as a silhouette. The farthest elements are de-emphasized by blurring the details.

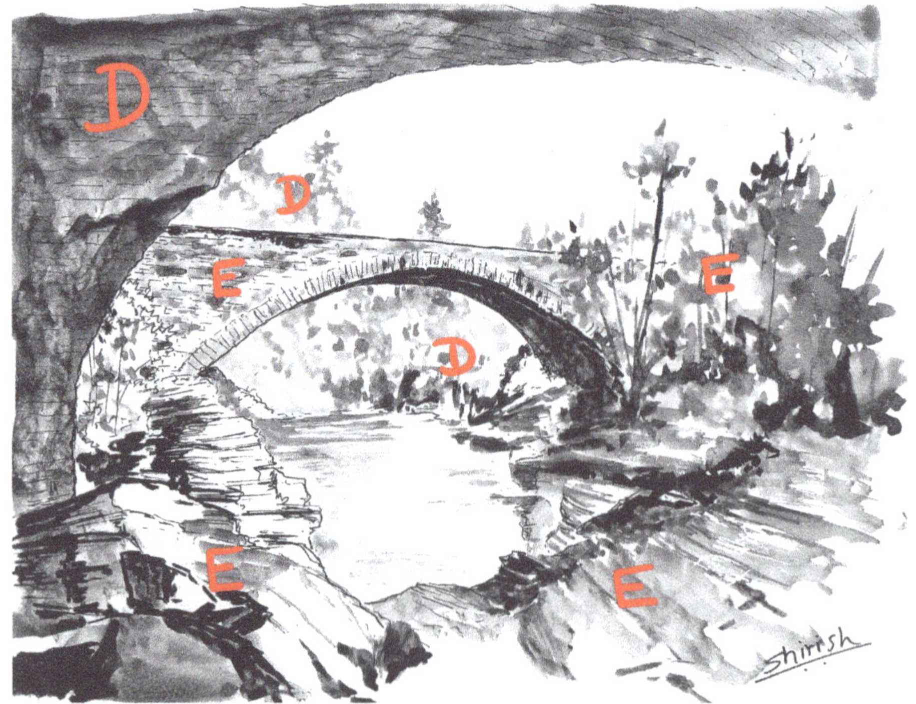

9. Using white space/ negative space/ empty space: You may observe that there are large white space blocks in the picture. But since they are placed side by side with the dark areas, our brain fills up the details and understands what these mean.

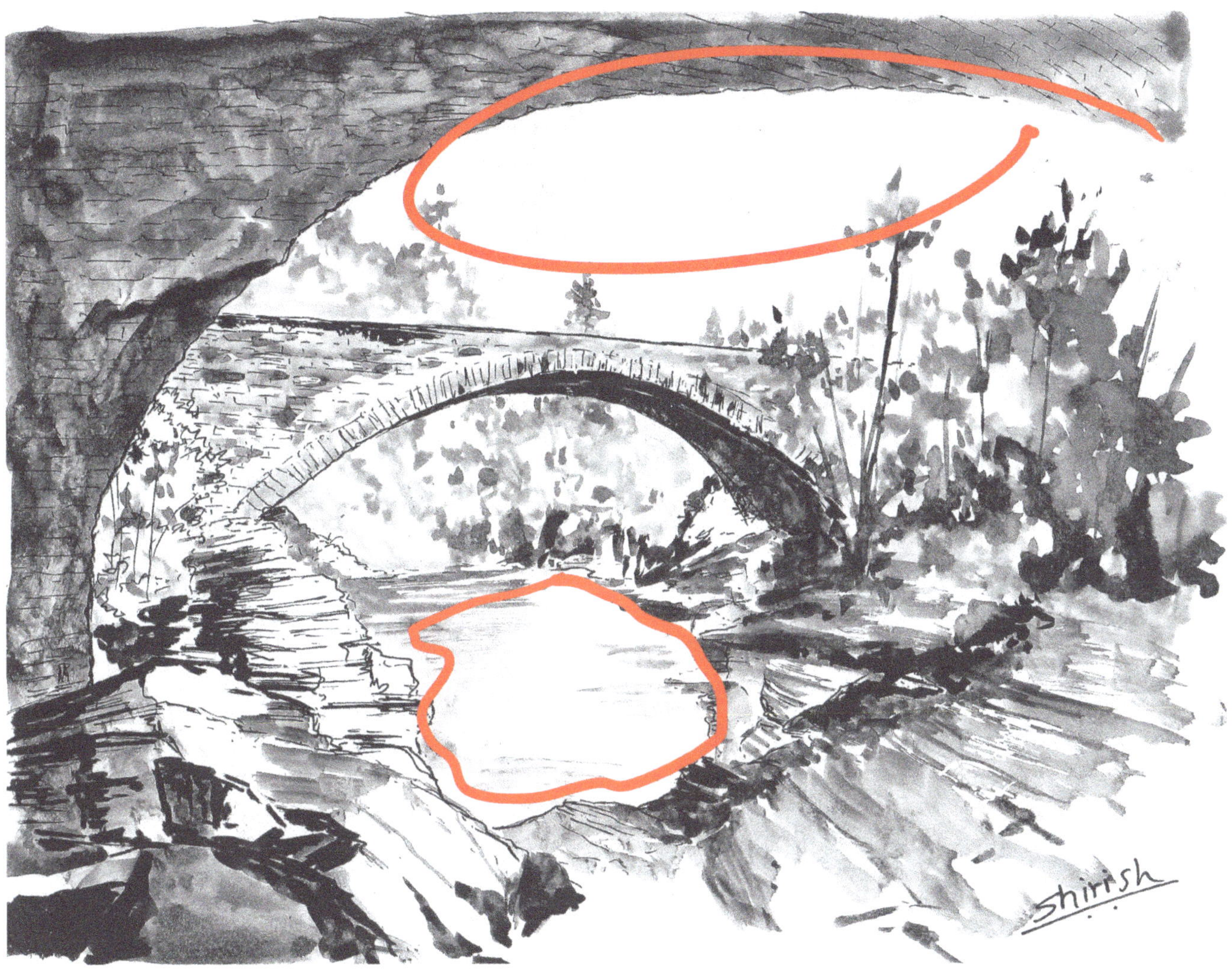

Now we are done with learning the 'rules' of the composition. Let's start with that mysterious entity called 'Perspective'.

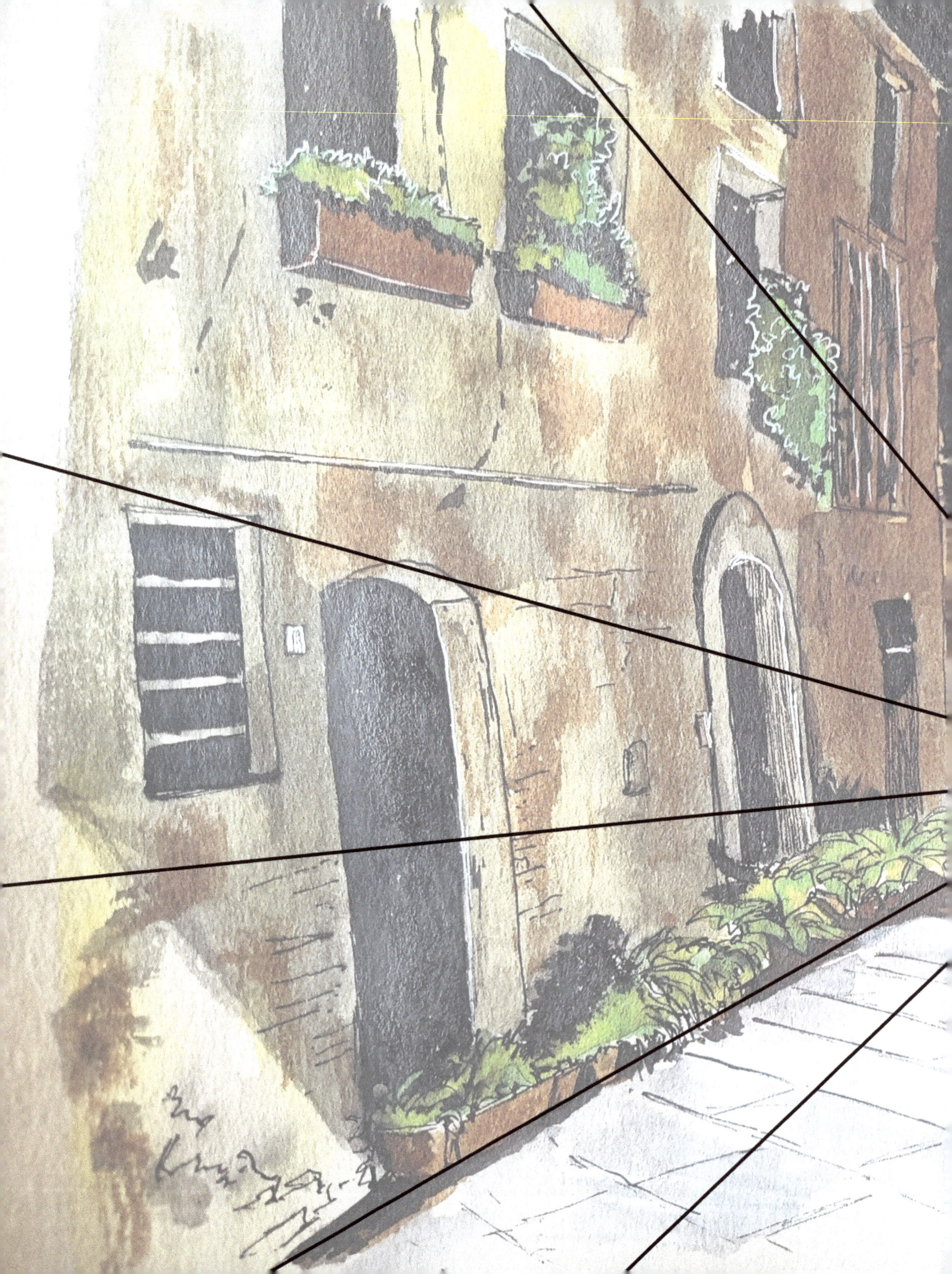

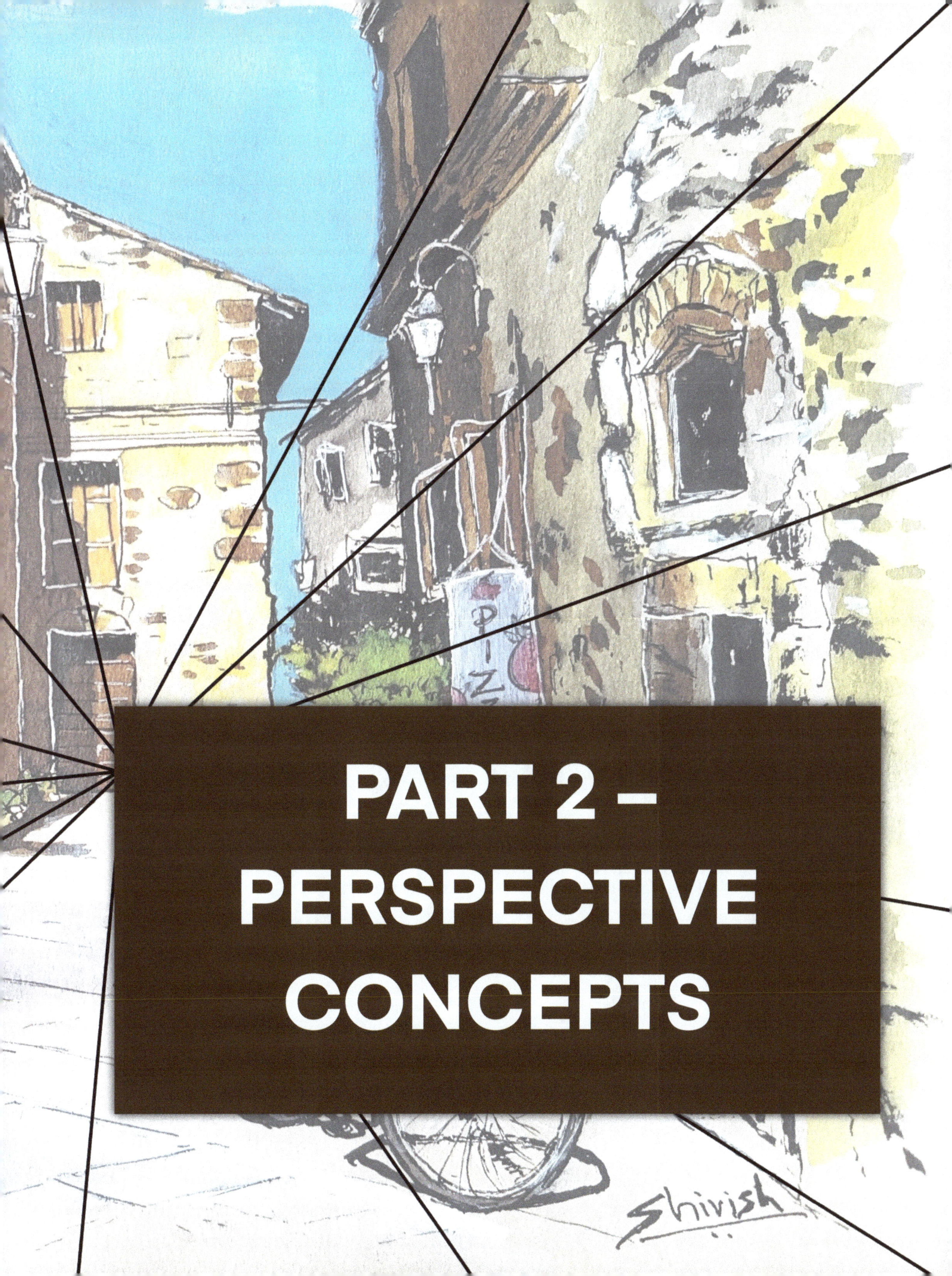

PART 2 –
PERSPECTIVE
CONCEPTS

What Is Perspective?

Perspective is the way one perceives something.

In plain English, perspective is the way one 'sees' something, as opposed to how that something actually 'is'.

'But isn't that the same? Isn't the way we see something is the same as what that something is?', you may ask.

I beg to differ.

Don't get me wrong here.

I am not saying what we see is 'Neo, take this Red Pill, and see how far the rabbit hole goes' different from reality!

If you have watched (and hopefully understood) 'The Matrix', you know what I mean.

If you haven't, the last line was not for you. Let's move on!

There are all kinds of factors which influence how we see and perceive elements around us.

Rather than lecture you further, I will show one example and tell you what I mean.

This (left) is John walking on a patch of grass. This picture shows how I see John.

Did you notice that bird the sky above?

This picture in the middle shows how the bird sees John.

The picture on the right shows how a poor ant in the grass saw John!

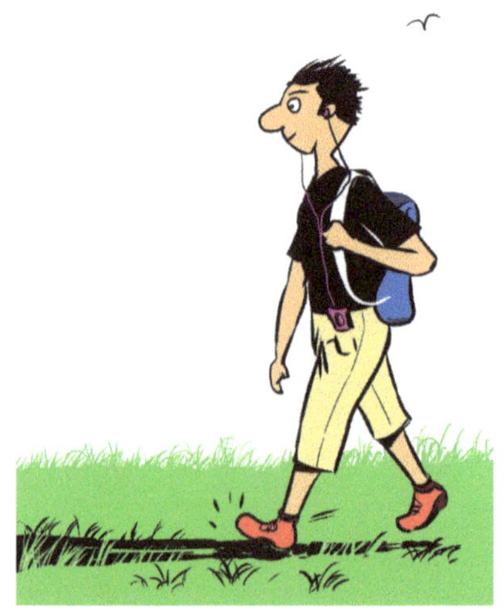 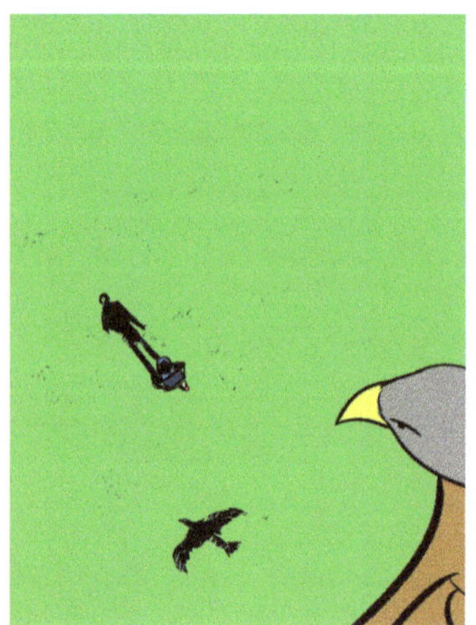 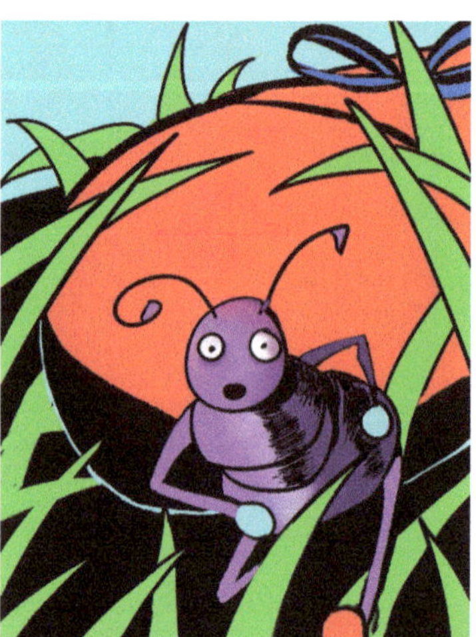

In the example above, you can see that it's the same person (John), and the same situation (John walking on the grass). But the way John and his situation is perceived is different for the different actors (Me, the bird and the ant).

Some of the factors influencing our perception are:

- The size of the element relative to us (Is it a small element like an ant, or a big element like an elephant, or a skyscraper, or a whale, or a T-Rex?).

- The amount, color and intensity of light falling on the element.

- Our distance from the element.

- The angle at which we are looking at the element.

And these factors I mentioned above are just the tip of the iceberg!

You got the drift, right?

As an artist, it's important for you to understand how these factors affect your perspective. Equally important is to incorporate these concepts into your artworks!

This will definitely make your artworks more appealing and believable for your viewers.

You may go a step further, bend and twist these principles to add some spice to your compositions. We will see some examples of how to do this later in this book.

Why Perspective Is Important?

Have you heard that ancient tale of seven blind people and an elephant?

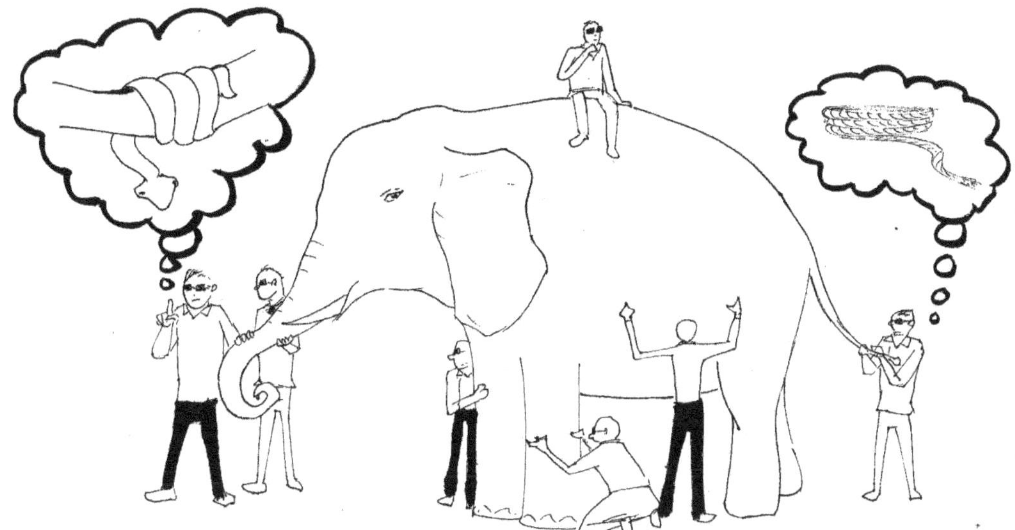

You haven't?

Let me enlighten you.

The tale is thus:

There were seven blind friends. While on their daily walk, they came across an elephant (don't ask me how!).

Since the elephant is a very big animal as compared to man, they had to scatter to feel their way around the elephant.

While passing around the elephant, some of them got hold of the elephant's legs.

One person got hold of the elephant's tail.

A couple of persons got hold of the elephant's trunk.

While one person landed near the elephant's head!

All the while, the elephant was standing dead quiet, not moving a muscle!

How did the one guy land near the elephant's head? And why did the elephant not move (or trampled them, for the violent types amongst you)?

How would I know?

I told you, this is an ancient tale. In this tale, the moral (or punchline) is more important than the logic!

So, where was I? Ohh yes...

Each one of the friends had got hold of one part of the elephant. None of them could see the whole elephant. So, they started guessing what they had stumbled upon.

The friends holding one of the legs of the elephant thought that they were holding on to a pillar.

The one guy who had landed near the elephant's head thought that he was sitting on a giant rock.

The one guy who held the elephant's tail thought that he was holding onto a hanging rope. (I hope he did not linger near that spot long enough to receive some nasty surprise!).

The poor guys who got hold of the elephant's trunk were scared witless, thinking they had laid their hands on a python!

If you are looking for the punchline, sorry to disappoint you. It ain't coming!

Yet, there's a moral.

Each one of these friends had limited knowledge of the situation. This limited knowledge shaped their radically different perspectives.

And their perspective was governed by their situation, not the reality.

Their situation included their place, and the part of the elephant they were holding. It never involved the entire elephant.

Cornerstones Of Perspective

There are several cornerstones of perspective:

a. Horizon

b. Picture plane

c. Distance, size and clarity

d. Distance and relative distance

e. Foreshortening

f. Vanishing point

Let's understand each one of these in detail.

Horizon

Horizon is the place where 'the world ends' for our vision.

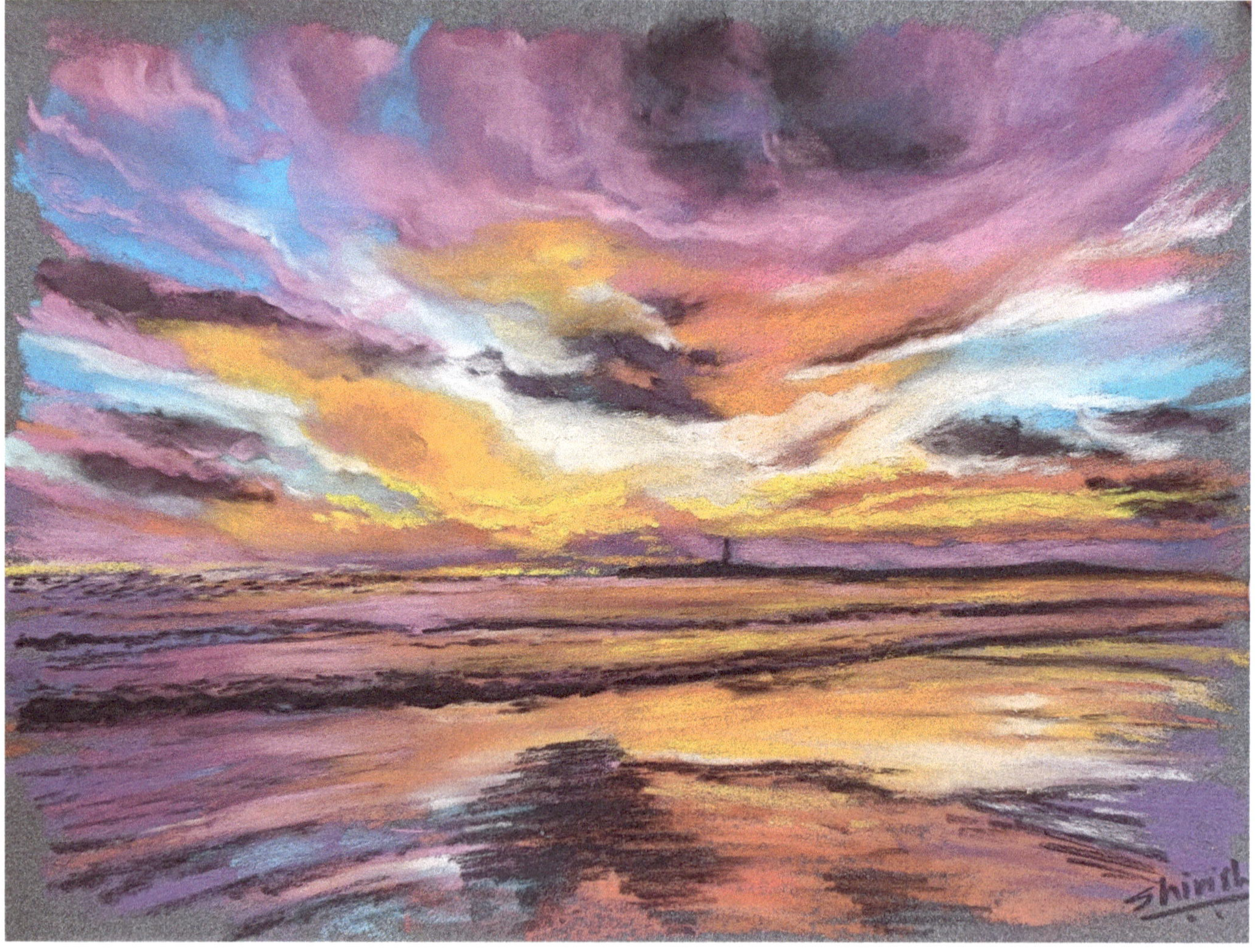

- Horizon is constant for a person… as long as he/she is not moving. A stationary place where a person is located is called 'Station Point'.

- When the person changes his/her station point, the reach of his/her vision changes. This changes the horizon line for that person.

For example, a person standing up can see farther than a person sitting down or lying down. A person standing over an elevated position (for example, on the top floor of a building/the top of a mountain), can see much further.

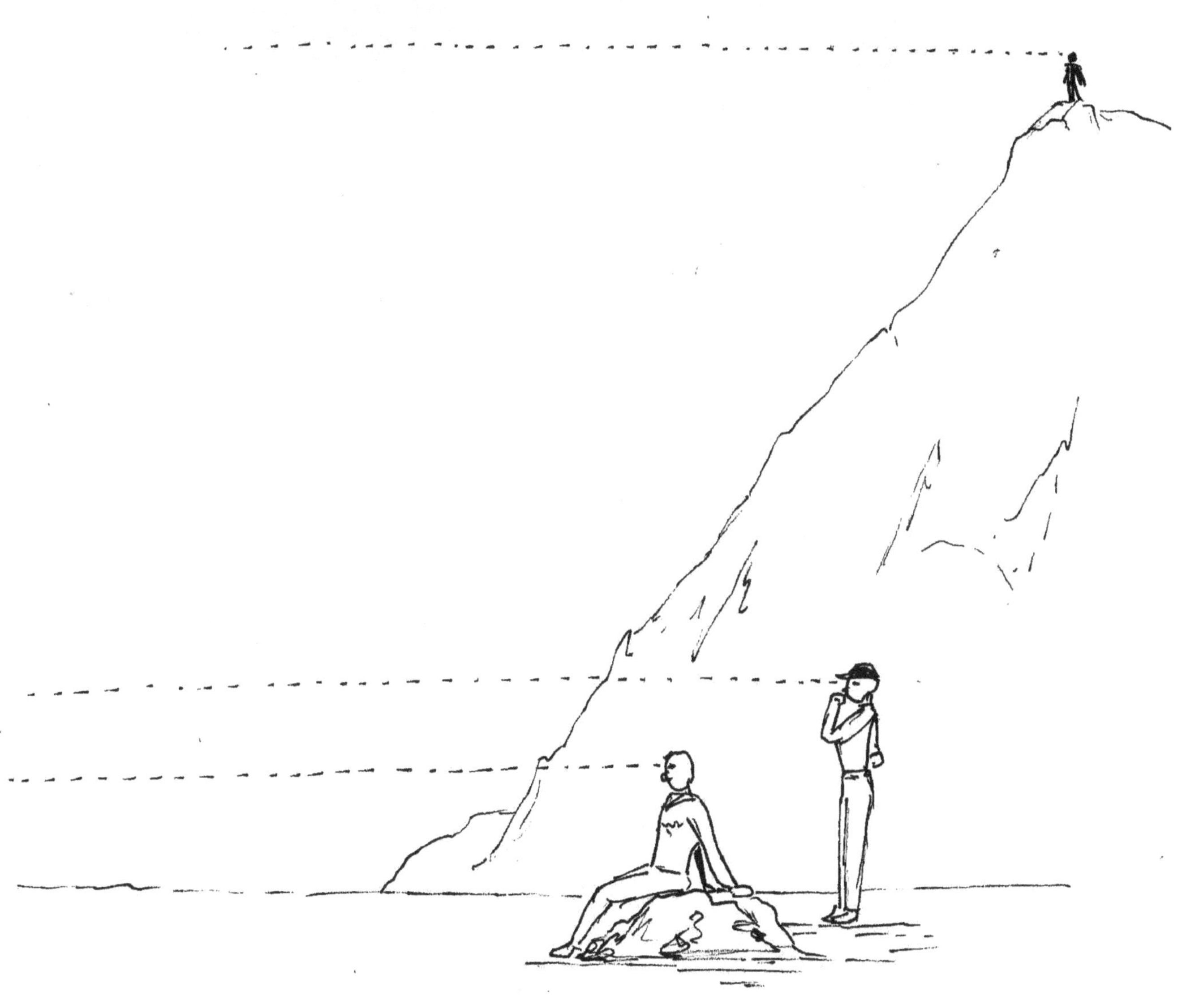

Picture plane (also called 'cone of vision')

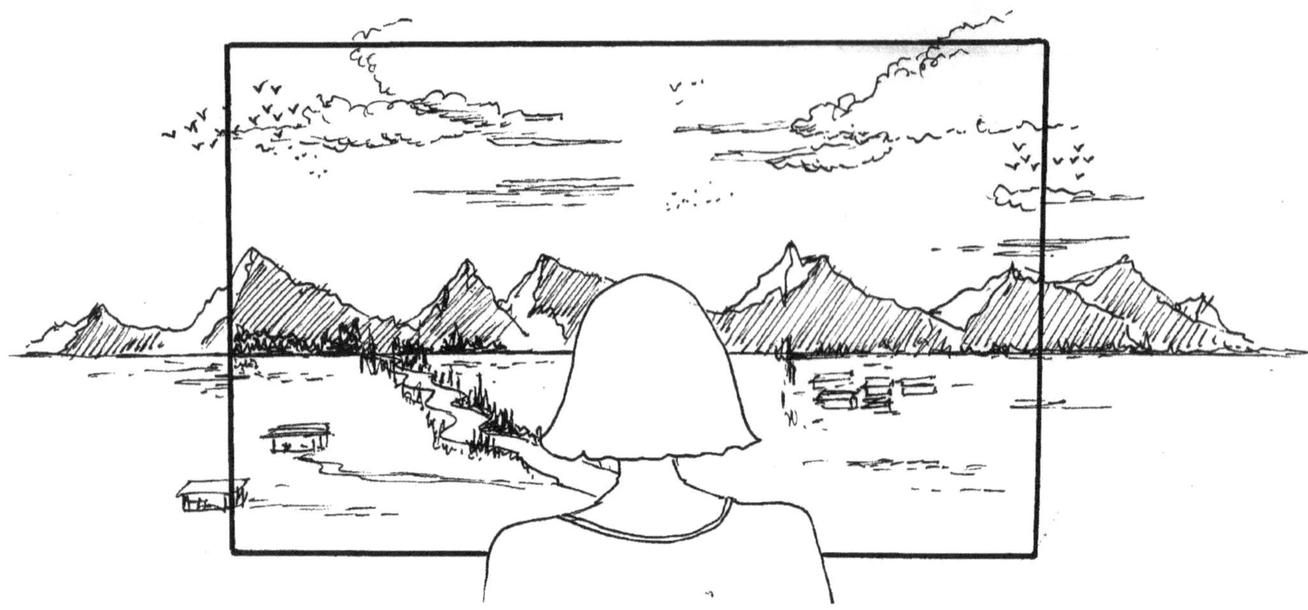

The picture plane is what we 'see'.

*   The picture plane is what is visible in a photograph/sketch.

*   You choose your picture plane while clicking a photograph/sketching.

*   Typically, a picture plane is represented as a rectangle, though it's not a rule. For example, if you are sketching/painting a picture on a round paper/canvas, your picture plane will be round.

The picture plane will obviously very when the person's position changes. It will also change when the elevation of the vision changes.

In plain English... when the person looks up, down or sideways, the picture plane will change.

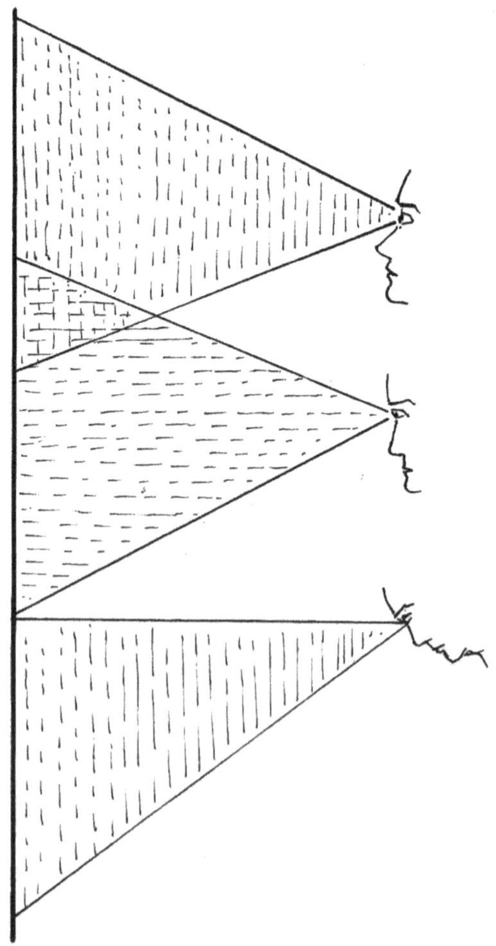

Composition and Perspective

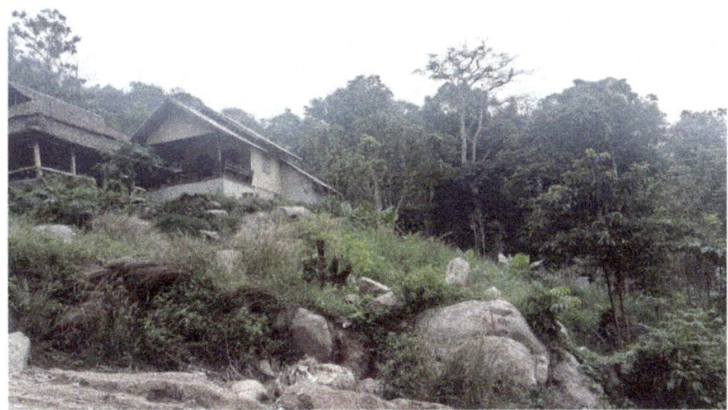

Let's see how the picture plane can vary for a picture even though the elements visible to the artist are the same.

On the left is a photograph I had clicked in one of my travels a few years ago. This photograph represents the picture plane that I saw while clicking it.

But I could have clicked the photograph of the same place like this…

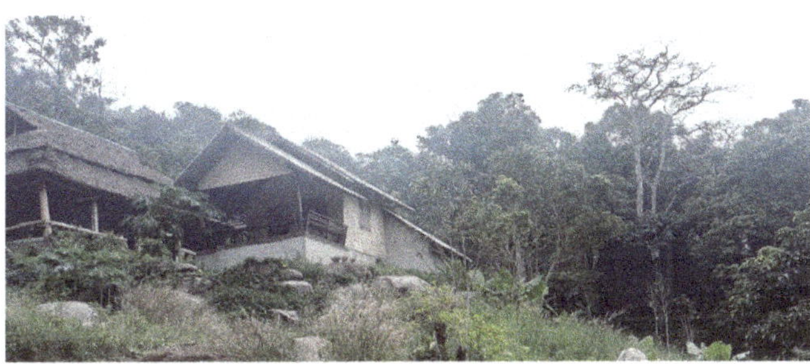

… or like one of these.

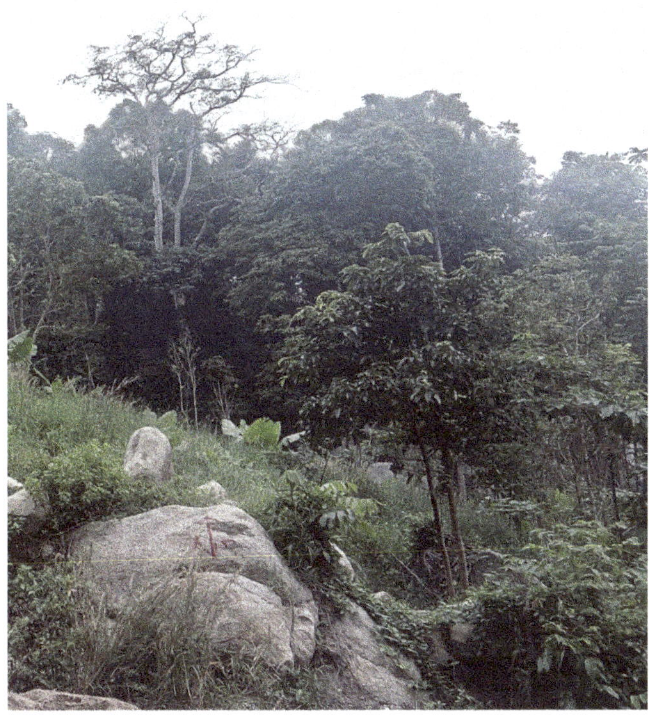

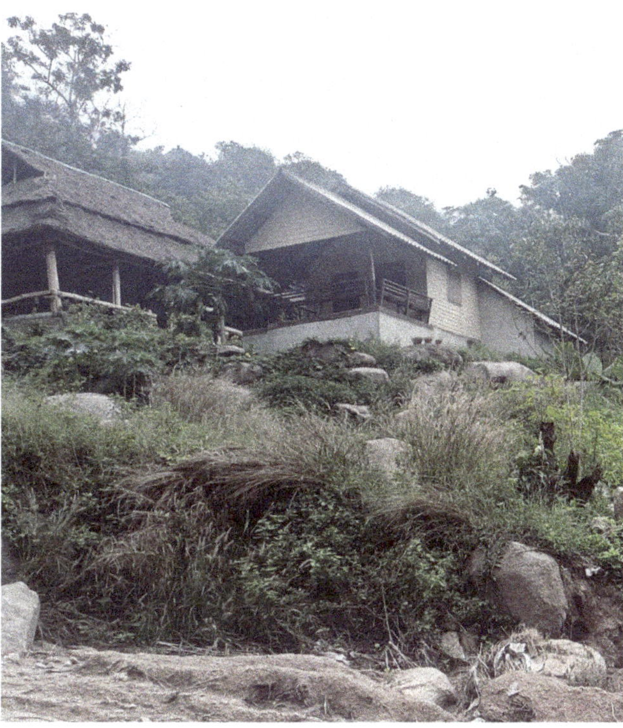

Moral of the story: The Picture Plane is what you see as an artist, and what you represent in your artwork.

Just make sure that once you have zeroed in on a picture plane, do not move it. Else all your proportions and perspective will go for a toss!

We will discuss vanishing point in a while. But before that, we need to learn some important concepts related to perspective.

Distance, size, and clarity (and aerial perspective)

We all know that elements closer to us appear bigger, while the elements distant to us appear smaller.

But have you observed that even the details of the elements which are distant to us are blurred?

This phenomenon (aerial perspective) is due to environmental factors like:

- Dust particles

- Moisture

- Light interference

- Pollutants

This blurring of details in distant elements can be used to a great effect to depict depth in the picture.

There are various methods in sketching to blur the distant elements. Some of them are as follows:

1. Use thick lines to outline the closer elements. Use thin lines / hatching lines / silhouettes / borderless figures for distant elements (first picture below).

2. Use bright colors for the elements closer to the viewer and muted/no colors for the distant elements (second picture below).

These are some of the methods of highlighting the distance of certain elements in a picture. Apart from these, you may come up with your own creative methods to depict distant elements.

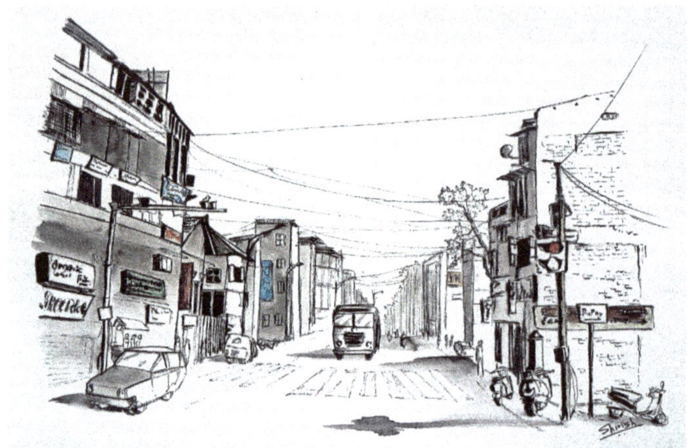

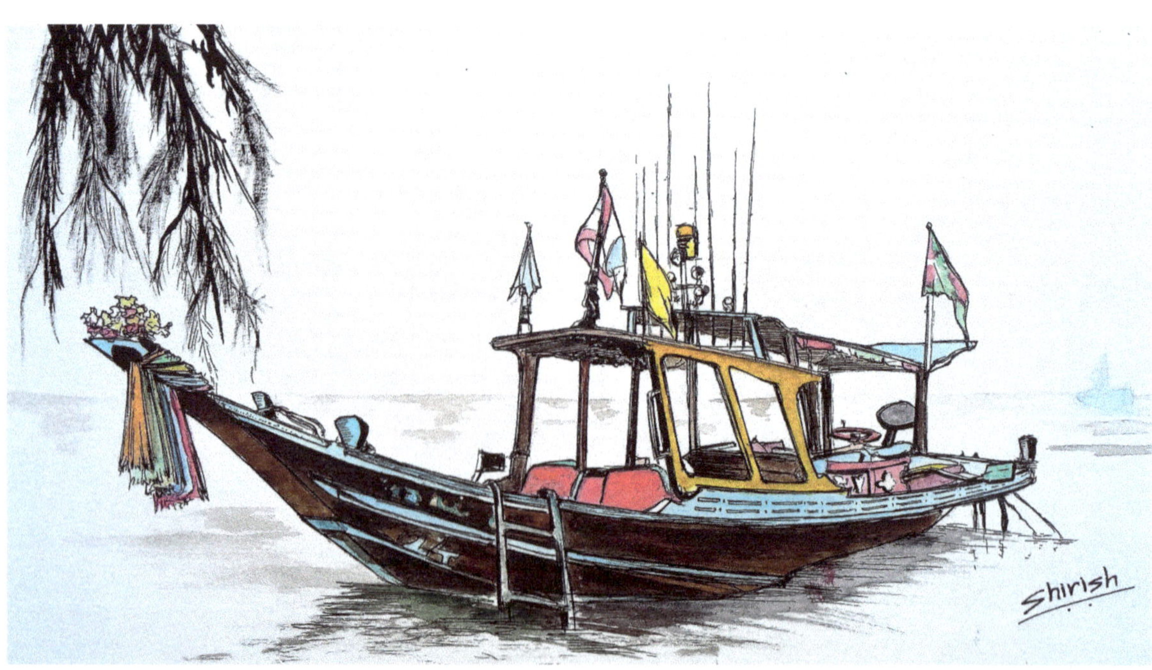

Composition and Perspective

Distance and relative distance

When elements are closer to the observer (aka us), the distance between them can be (nearly) correctly guessed.

However, when the elements are further away from

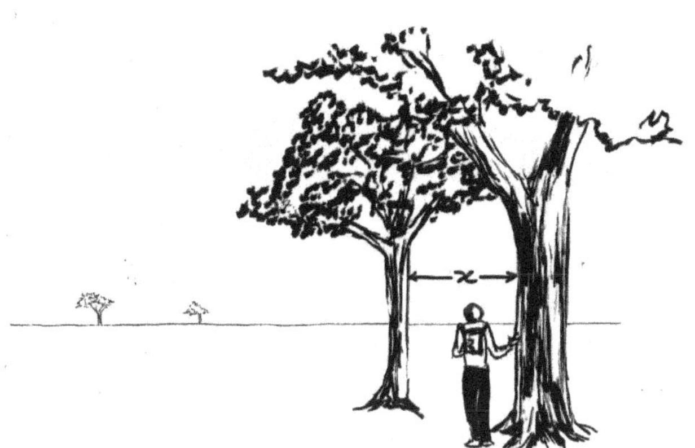

If we move closer to those trees, we will observe the distance increasing between them.

This is the same reason that celestial bodies appear to be a few meters away from each other to our eyes. But in reality, these stars and galaxies may be light years apart.

Still not convinced?

Let's think of an analogy.

Assume that a very poor, homeless person is suddenly offered a couple of grands.

On the house. Complimentary. No strings attached.

How will he/she feel?

Ecstatic? Elated? Top of the world? In the seventh heaven?

Can you think of more such words?

us, we tend to misjudge the relative distance between them.

How? Let's see with an example:

Here's a person standing very close to two trees. He can see the two trees at a distance of say 'x' from each other.

Now, look at the two trees wayyyyy back towards the horizon.

Does the distance between these two distant trees appear the same as the distance between the two nearer trees?

But, in reality, these two trees at the horizon may be miles apart from each other. They appear closer because they are distant to us.

Go on, let's see how far you can stretch your English. I am waiting.

No more words? Hmm… okay then.

Now let's offer those same two grands to a BILLIONAIRE!

On the house. Complimentary. No strings attached.

Will he/she care? I don't really know since I am not a billionaire (yet!). However, my wild guess is a resounding 'no'. Not really.

Why?

Because it's not important how much amount you are offering someone. It's more important what that person already has! What he/she has will decide the magnitude of what he/she is receiving from the perspective of that person.

Everything is relative, and so is perspective!

Foreshortening

There's a saying in the Sales and Marketing world.

People have two reasons when they say 'no' to a sale... a reason which is real, and a reason which sounds good!

Similarly, when people look at any element, there are two shapes to that element... a shape which is real, and a shape which is foreshortened.

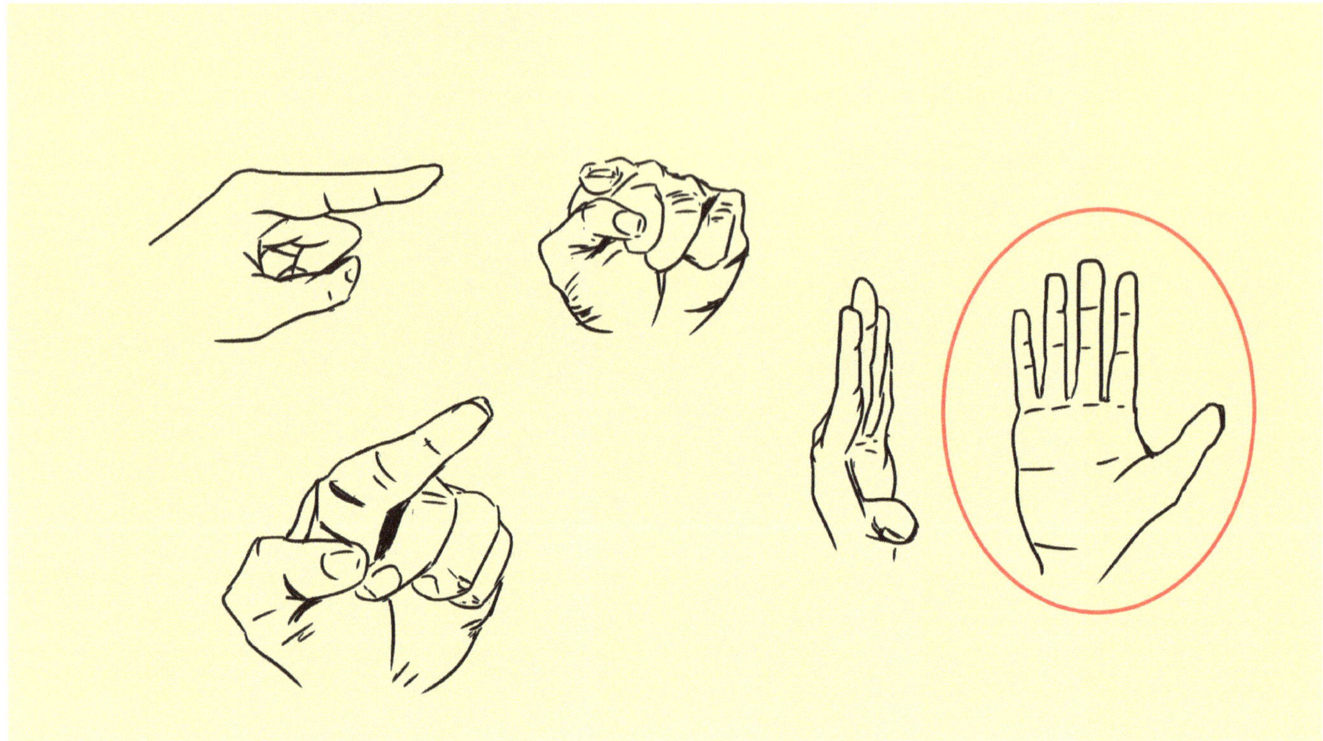

What the heck is foreshortened?

When we look at an object, the object's shape may appear somewhat skewed/distorted. The amount of distortion will depend on the angle at which we are looking at that object.

Only at one specific angle can we really see the object as it is, while it's very distorted at certain other angles. Look at the illustration of a hand in various positions above. The hand position marked inside a circle is the only one where the hand looks as-is to us.

On the right are some of the examples of the objects of daily use appearing foreshortened.

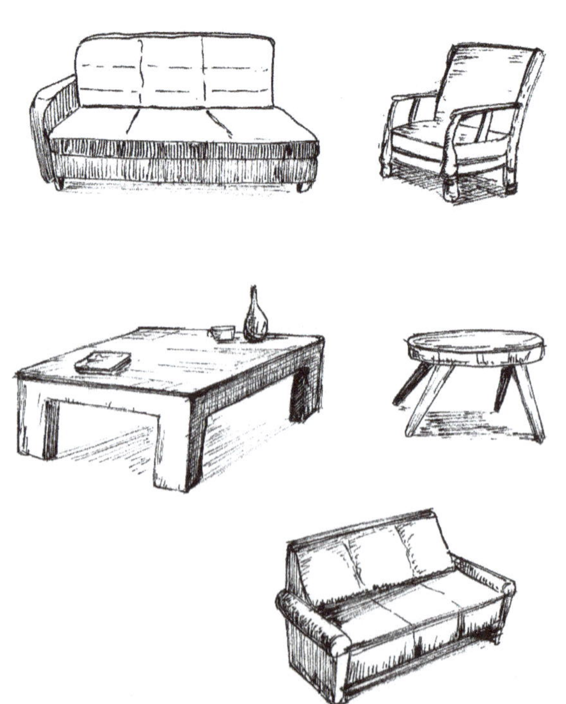

Vanishing point

As promised, we have now (finally) arrived at the vanishing point.

A vanishing point is a point where a set of parallel lines appears to meet.

Note that these lines are parallel, and never actually meet. But to our vision, they appear to converge at a point.

Why?

As the distance between these lines and us increases, we perceive the distance between them to be getting smaller and smaller. And at one point, we perceive them to meet.

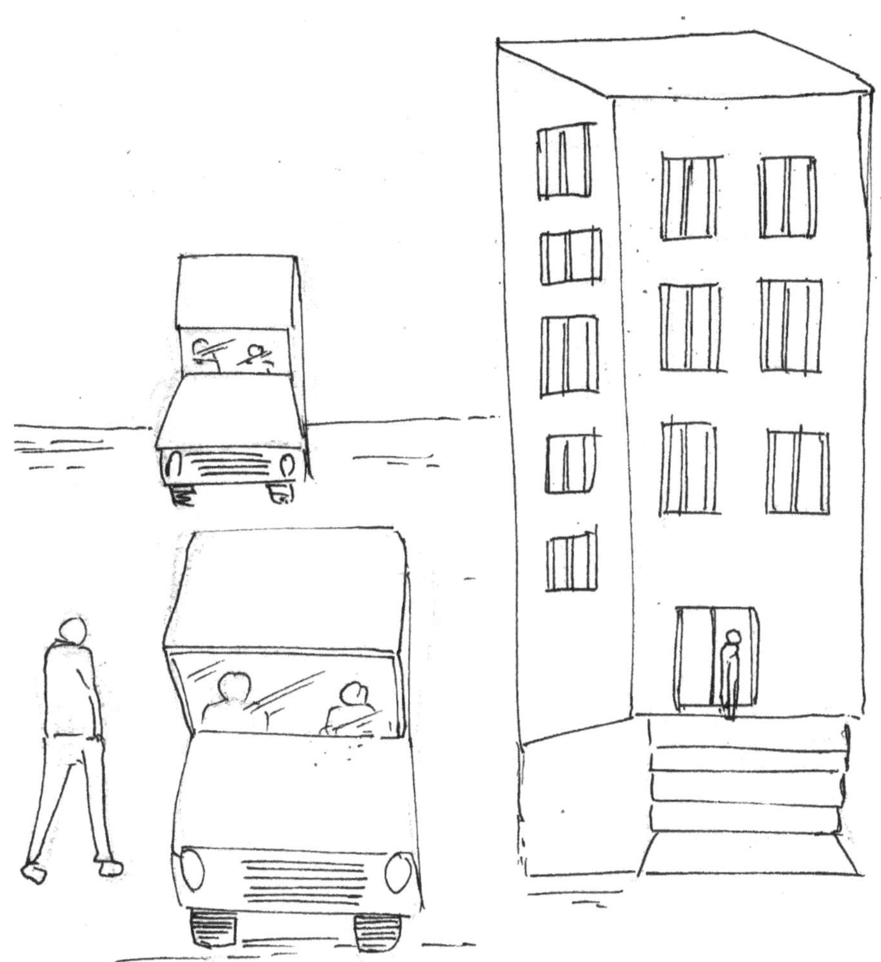

So what? How does it affect your sketches?

Let's see one example of a sketch, where the perspective has gone wrong! This is a somewhat extreme case of the wrong perspective. But it's included here to make an important point.

This wrong perspective is the result of incorrectly calculating the vanishing point.

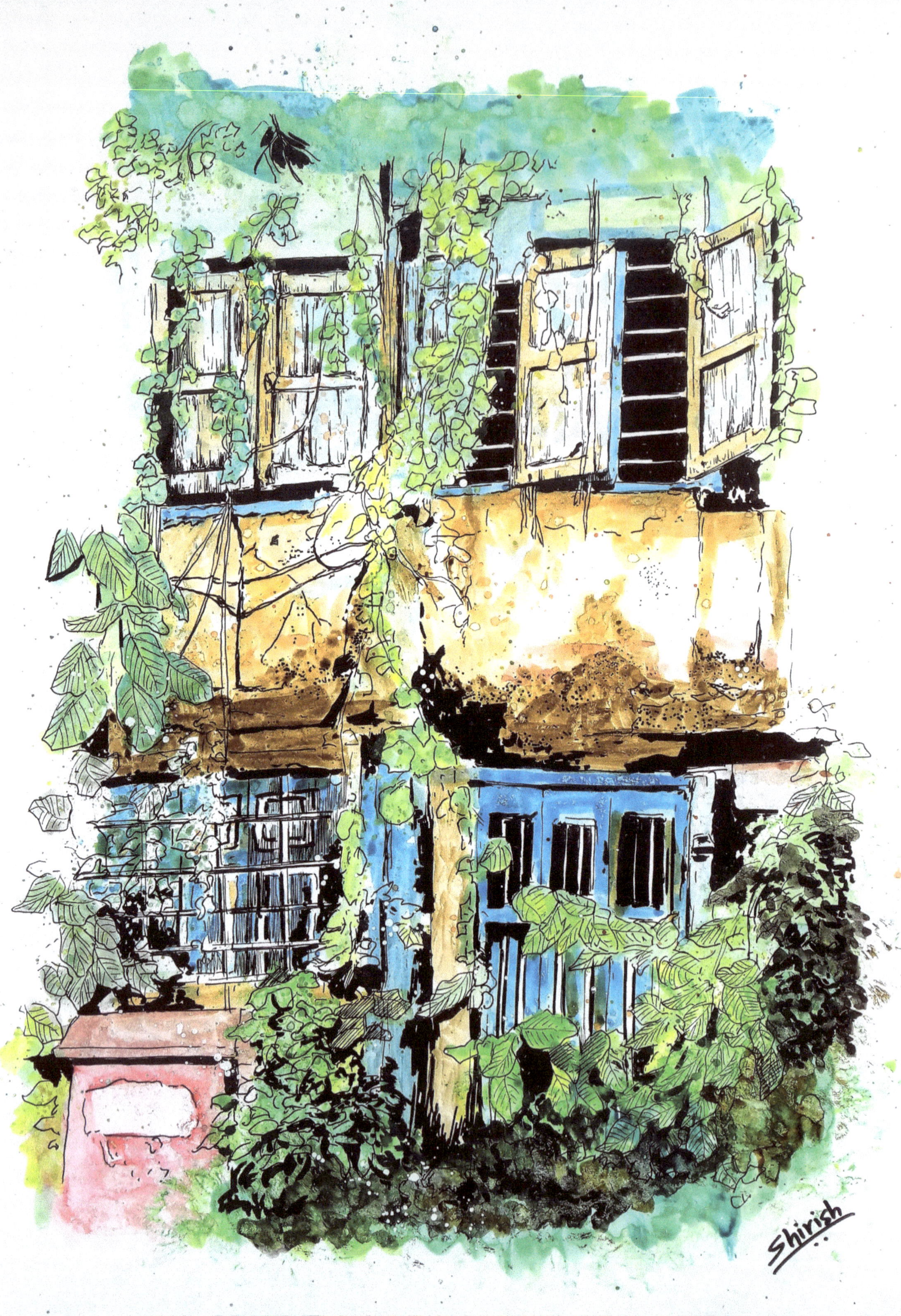
Shirish

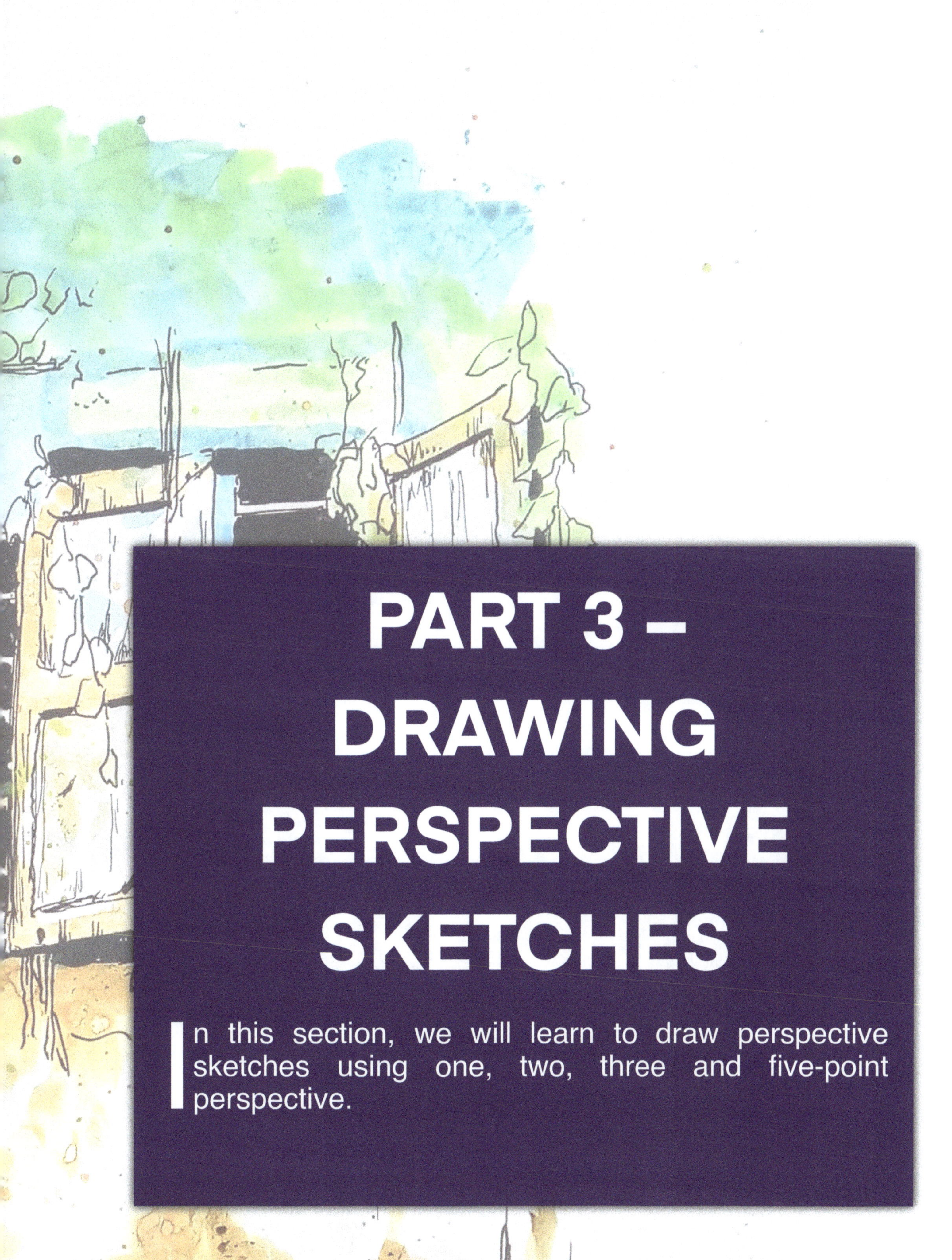

In this section, we will learn to draw perspective sketches using one, two, three and five-point perspective.

Bonus: Want to see how the picture on the previous page was sketched? Head over to this URL:

https://youtu.be/tb755dLU9c0

(or use the QR code given below) to watch the complete video of the making of this sketch. And don't forget to subscribe to the channel!

One-point perspective

As the name indicates, there's only one vanishing point in these pictures.

All the lines going away from viewer converge into this one vanishing point.

We see this kind of perspective all around us every day. Most photographs of people/photographs captured from the front are in one-point perspective.

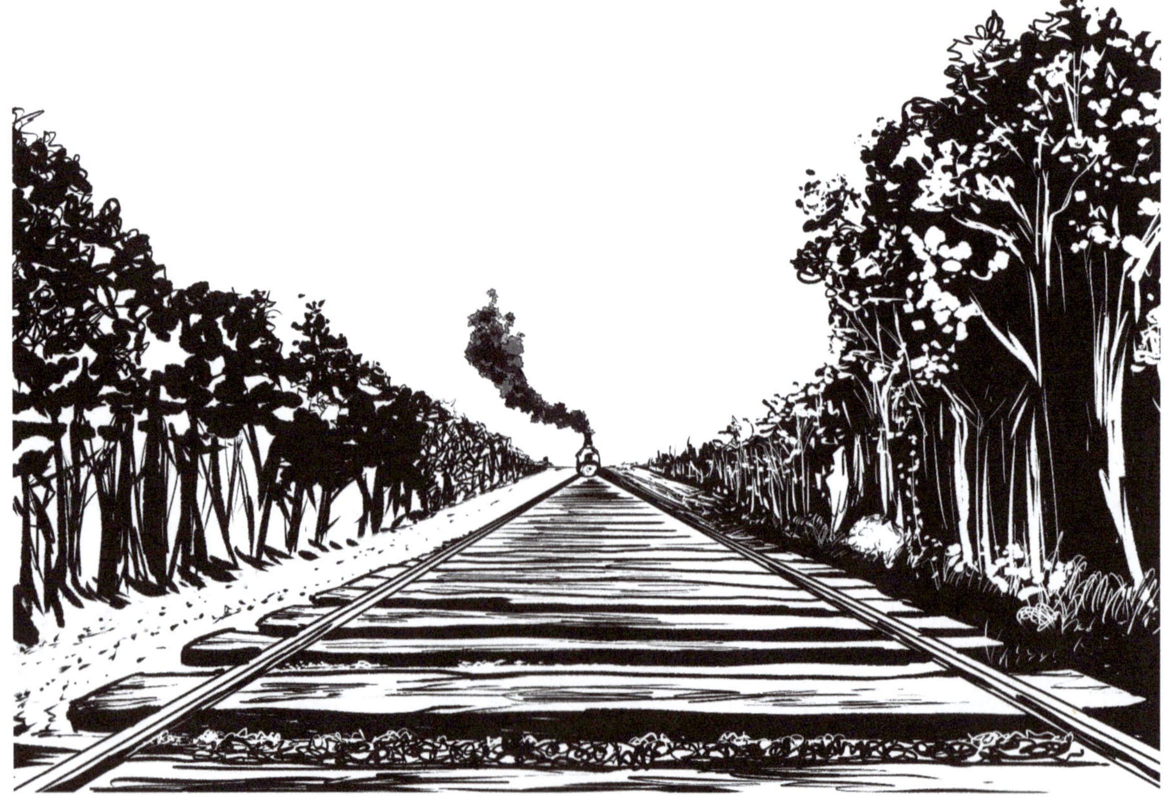

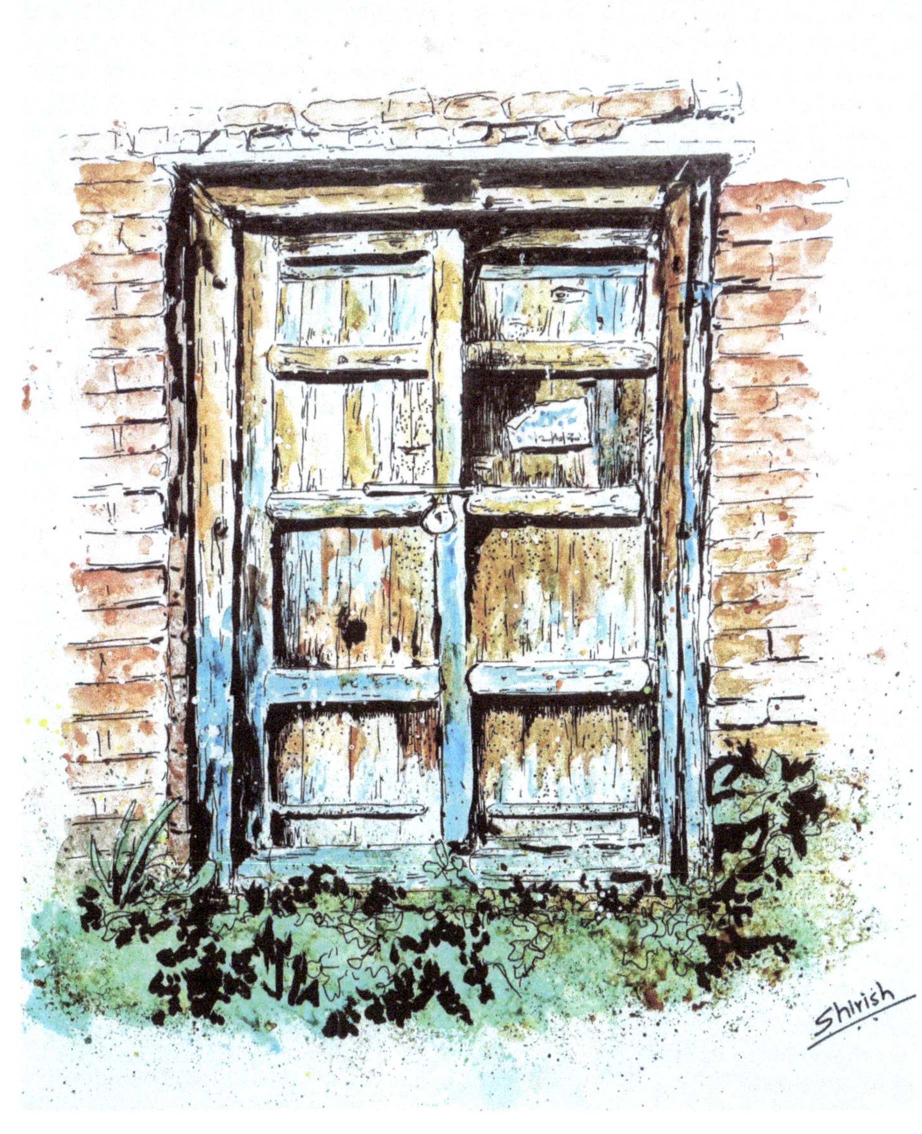

While drawing a scene with one-point perspective, remember the following key guidelines:

1. The vanishing point is always, always on the horizon line. No exceptions!

Note: In almost all the obvious examples used to show the one-point perspective, the vanishing point is always shown in the center. This is done for the ease of understanding.

However, in real life, the vanishing point can be anywhere over the horizon line. Within or outside the picture plane.

See the picture below to understand what I mean.

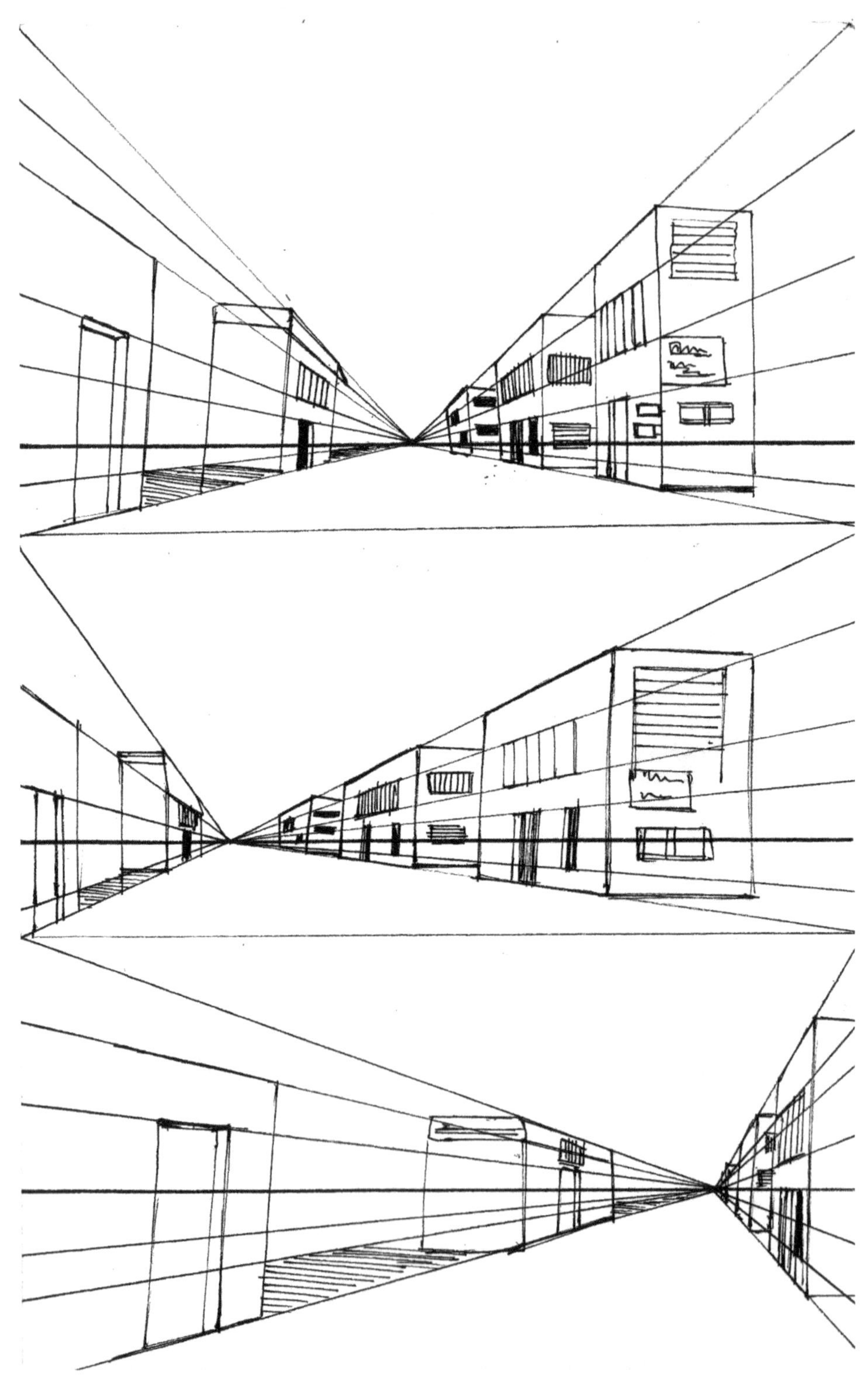

Composition and Perspective

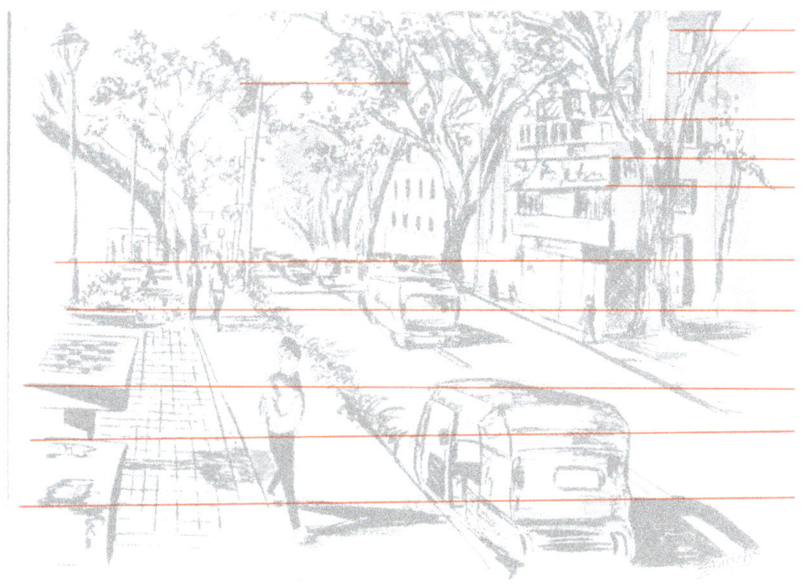

2. All the horizontal lines remain parallel to the horizon.

3. All the vertical lines remain perpendicular to the horizon.

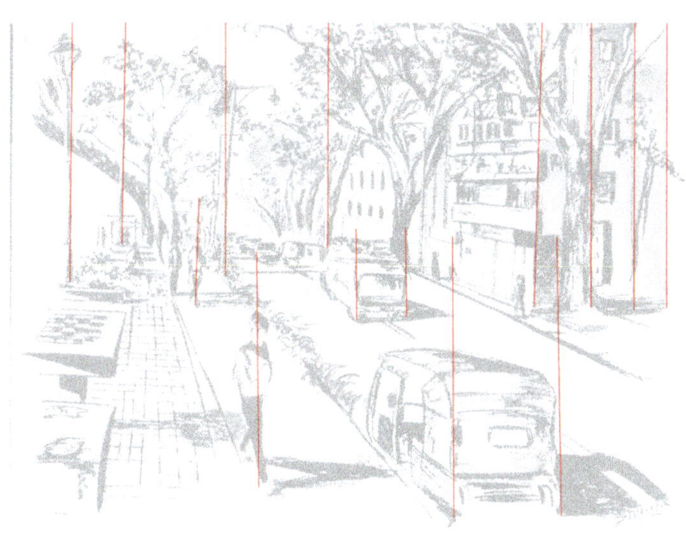

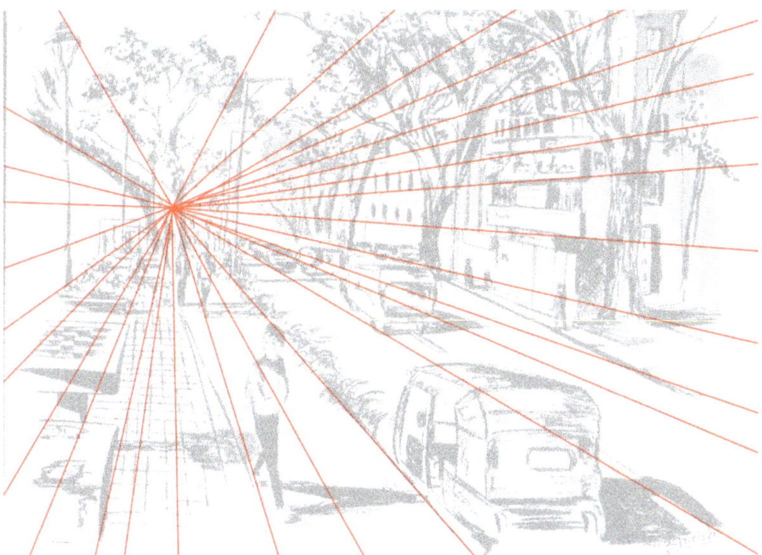

4. The lines which travel from the viewer to the vanishing point converge into the vanishing point.

5. As the consecutive horizontal and vertical lines move towards the vanishing point, the distance between the successive lines will appear to reduce. This is due to the 'relative distance' property we learned earlier.

In the picture on the right, observe how the distance between the successive light poles appears to be decreasing as they are placed further away from us.

With the above guidelines in mind, let's draw a quick sketch using one-point perspective.

We will start with the example photograph below. This is one of those ideal photographs to study one-point perspective, because:

a) The lines are all straight.

b) The picture contains all artificial objects. These artificial objects have straight lines and no random shapes like foliage.

These kinds of photographs are ideal for starting out with one-point perspective.

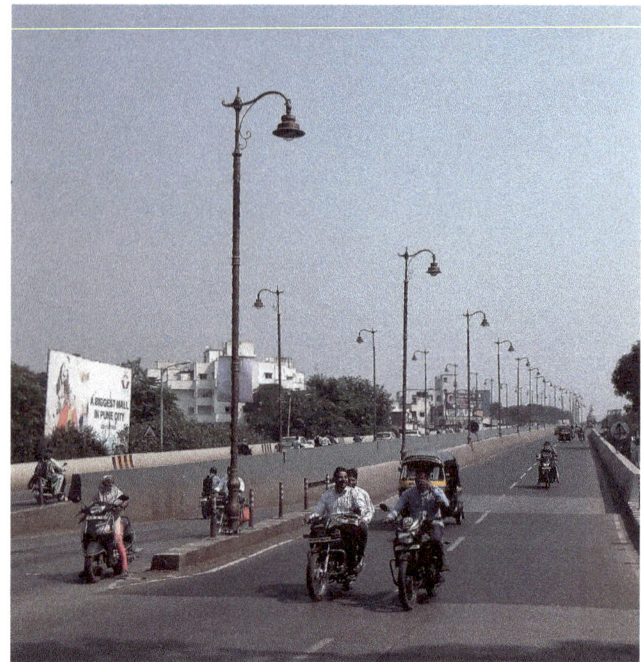

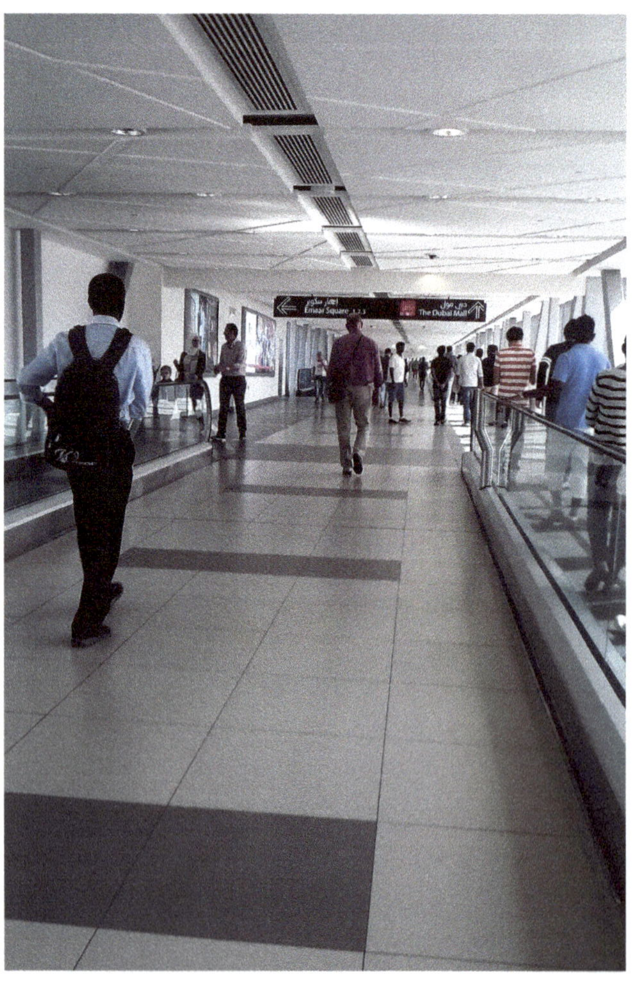

When doing a live sketch/on-site sketch, I always try to find a nice, comfy spot. I should be able to stand/sit at this spot without moving until I am done with the sketch. This spot is called 'the station point'.

Even if you do half the sketch standing up and half of it sitting down, your perspective will go wrong. When you change your station point, your picture plane, and horizon changes.

So, once you identify your picture plane and horizon, stick to it.

When I need to move away from my station point during a sketch, I make sure to click a photograph of the subject. This helps me conserve the original perspective from which I had started.

As we are drawing from a photograph here, our station point will always be fixed. So, that's one less thing to worry about!

First, we will identify the horizon line. The horizon line may differ as per your position.

How do we find the horizon line in such a crowded scene, as the actual horizon is not visible here?

For that, we use our eye level.

When I see a person having about the same height as me, I see the top of his/her head at the horizon line. But while clicking this photograph, the camera was at my chest level. If I had kept the camera at my eye level, I would see all the heads touching the horizon.

Composition and Perspective

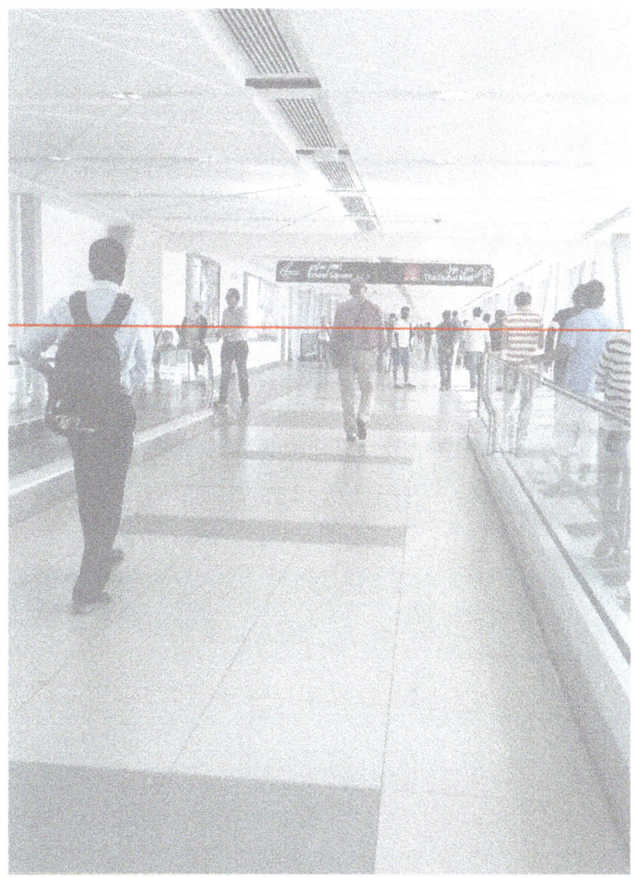

How many converging lines should you draw? Totally depends on your gut feel. I suggest drawing 8-10 lines for the start and then adding them as required later.

Now draw horizontal lines (next page). As we move towards the vanishing point, the distance between consecutive lines should keep reducing.

Is there a mathematical formula for calculating this reduction in the distance?

Yes, there is.

Are we going to discuss this formula in this book?

Absolutely not!

So, the horizon is at the chest level of most of the people in this photograph.

Now that we have identified our horizon, let's find the vanishing point.

When the vanishing point is decided, we start drawing the converging lines. These lines should be drawn from the vanishing point to the corners of the page.

Since this photograph already has many converging lines, it makes our task very easy.

Refer to the picture below. Start with the uppermost lines. These lines should extend from the vanishing point to the upper corners of the frame.

Then draw similar lines which extend from the vanishing point to the lower corners of the frame.

Keep these lines extremely light. They are meant for our reference, not to show to the viewer.

Now start drawing in-between converging lines to the extreme lines already drawn.

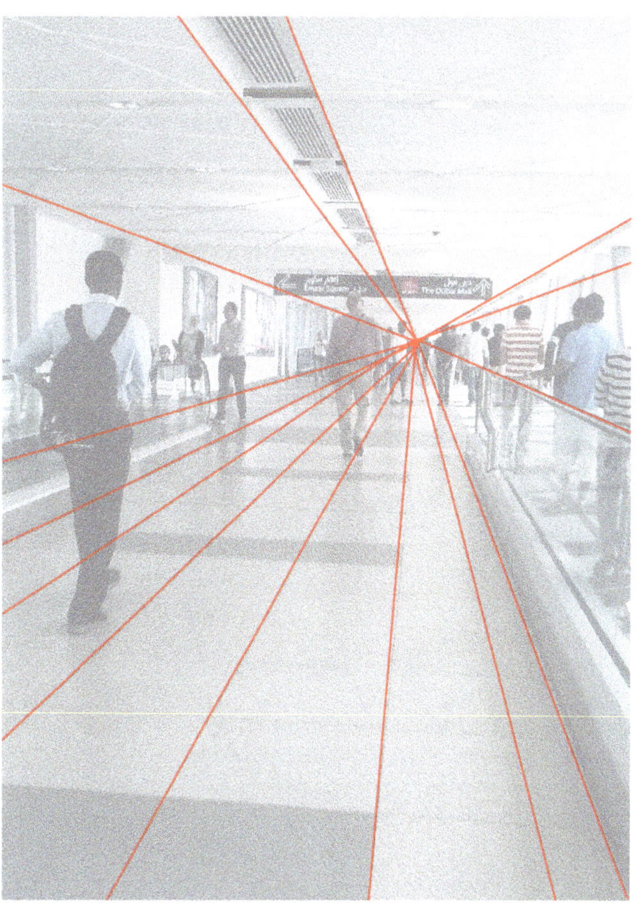

As I have categorically specified earlier, this is not an architectural perspective book. We go purely by our gut feel here.

Just like converging lines, the number of horizontal lines depends on your gut feel. We can always add/remove lines as needed once we start drawing.

Now draw vertical lines (below). Keep decreasing the distance between the consecutive vertical lines as we move towards the vanishing point.

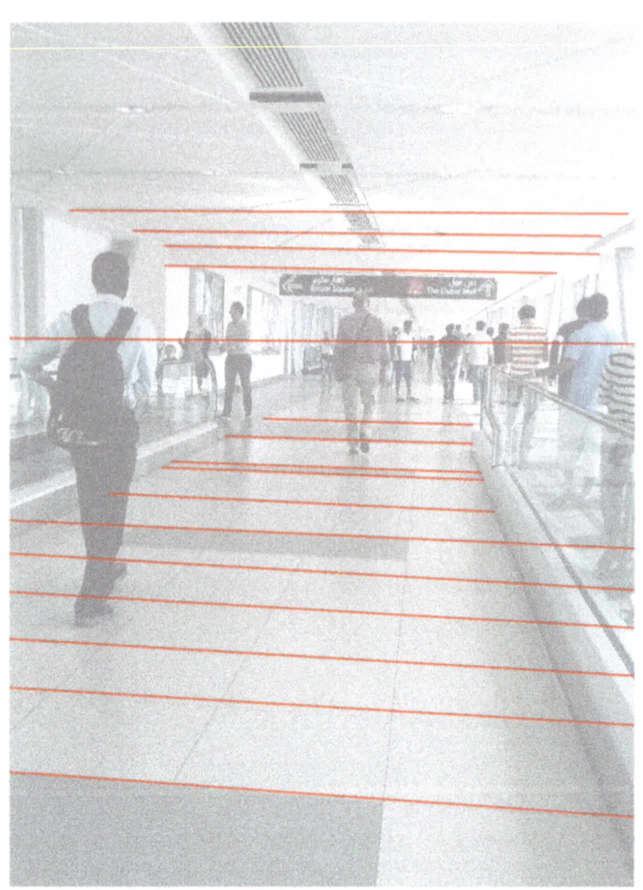

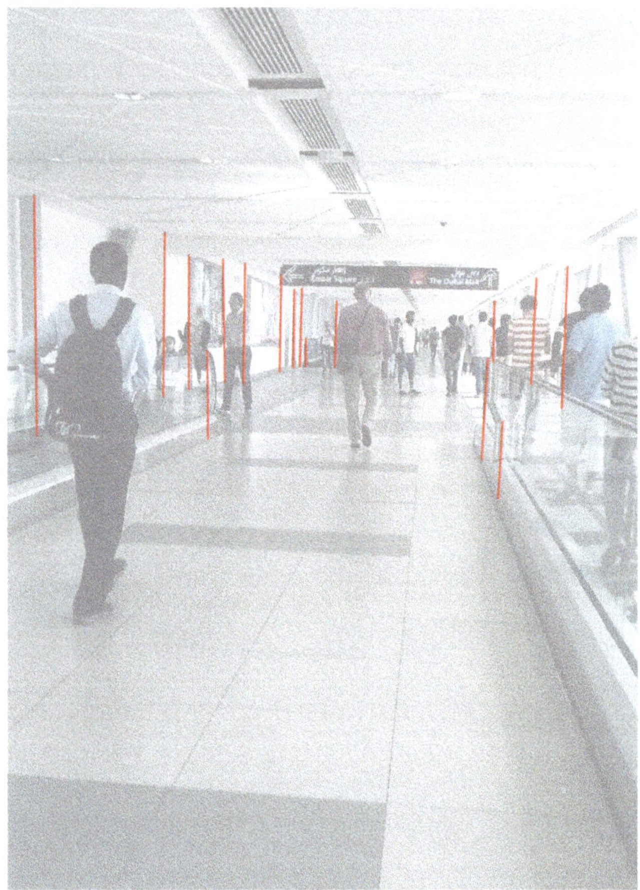

Now our framework for drawing one-point perspective sketch is ready. Let's go ahead and turn it into a sketch.

Keep as closely aligned as possible to the perspective lines, but do not be very fussy. We are not doing an architectural drawing here.

On the right is the sketch that was done using with the perspective lines as shown above.

On the next page is the same sketch along with the perspective lines. This will make it easier to understand. See how the various elements are aligned with the perspective lines.

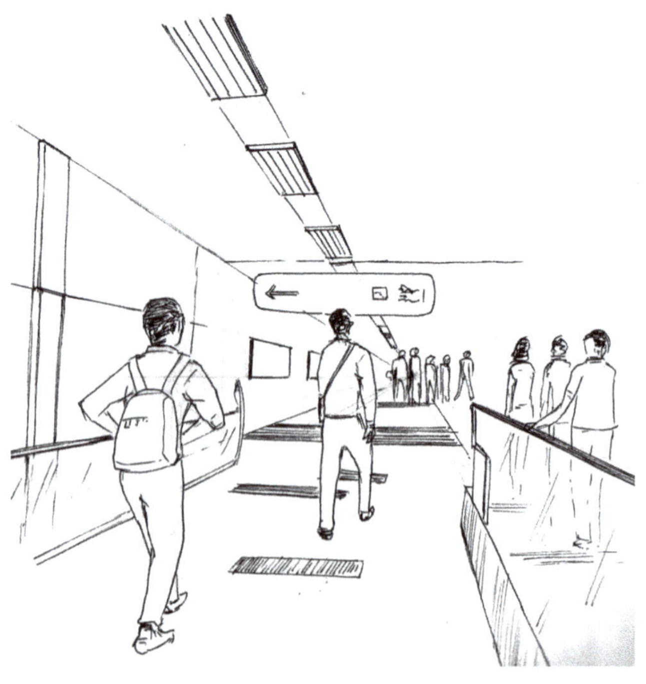

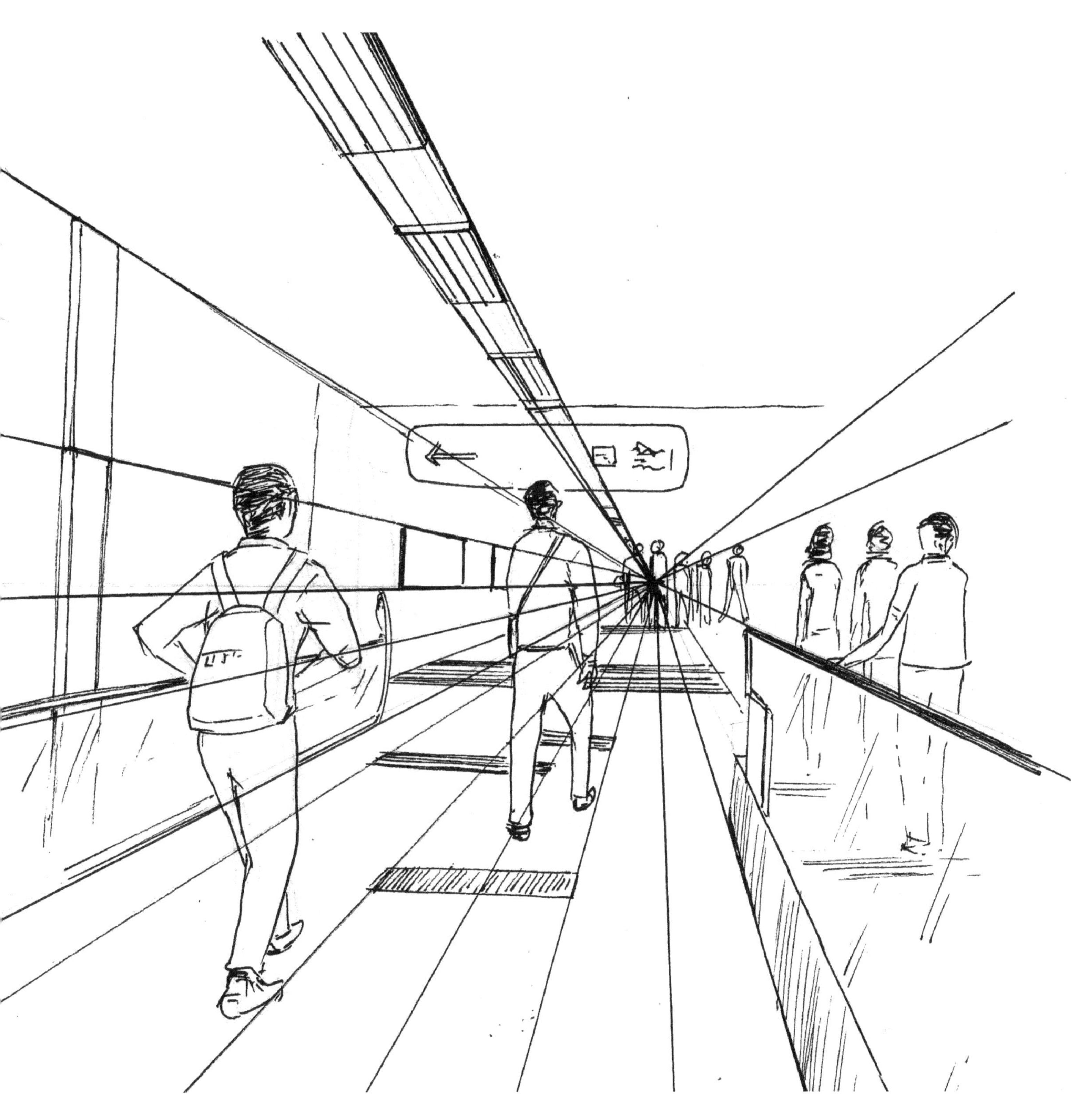

One-point perspective - Curves and challenges

Till now, we discussed some of the pretty straightforward examples of the one-point perspective.

But in real life, you will seldom come across such simple situations.

So, we will cover 2 situations where the one-point perspective is a little tricky.

In the example below, the area near the vanishing point suddenly curves, instead of being confined to straight vanishing lines.

How do we cope-up with this situation?

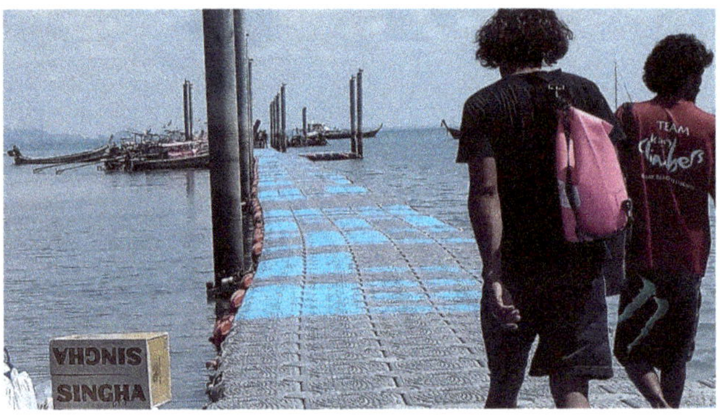

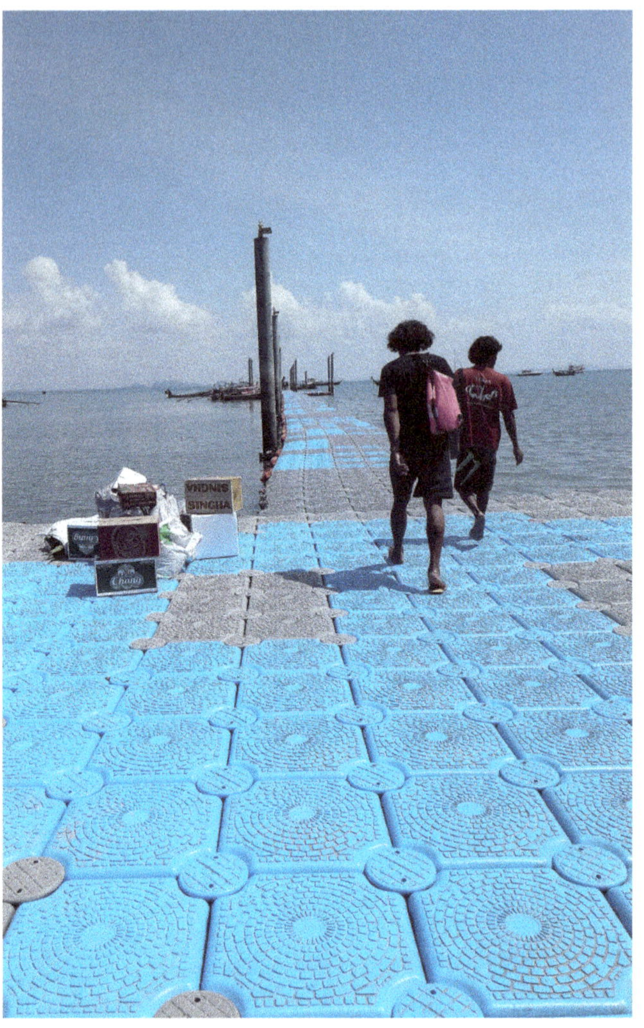

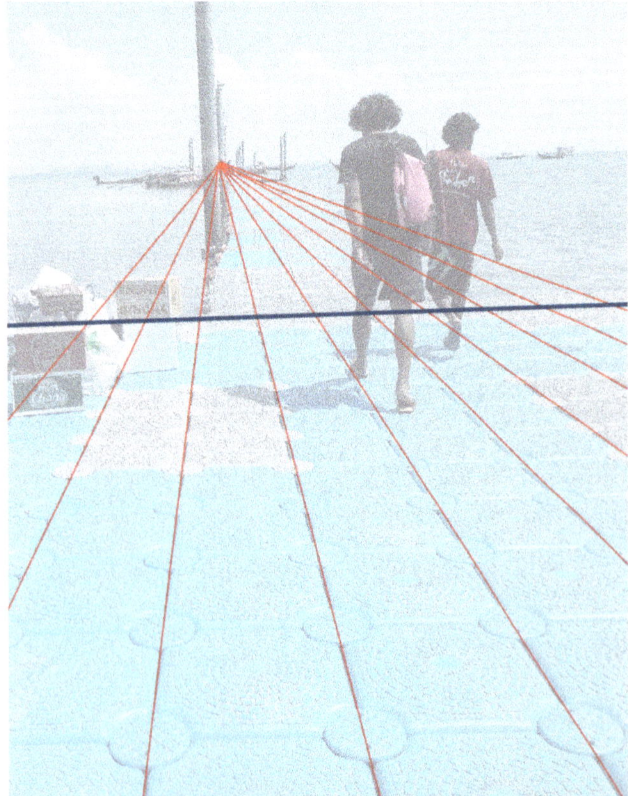

First, we assume that everything is in a straight line, and draw converging lines and the horizon. See the picture to the left to understand what I mean.

A horizontal line separates the picture into two parts.

Below this horizontal line, all lines are straight. Above this line, the path curves.

Composition and Perspective

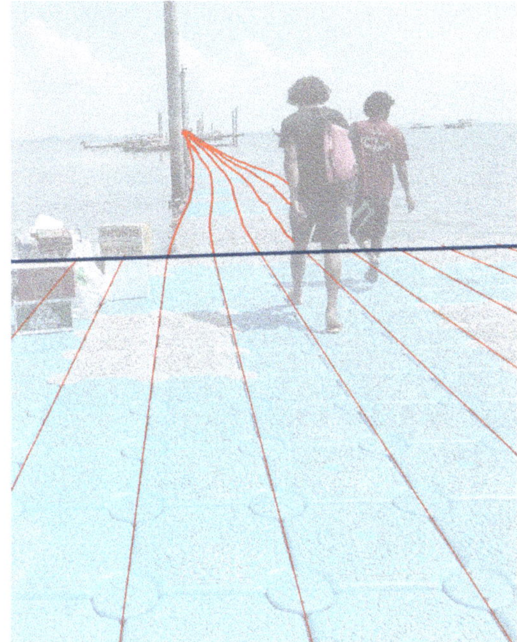

We can treat the part below this horizontal line in the same way as a 'normal' one-point perspective picture and draw the tiles.

For the picture above the horizontal line, we will use the same vanishing point, but draw curved perspective lines as shown to the left.

Note that these curved lines are ultimately merging with the straight lines.

The horizontal and vertical lines will be completely unaffected by these antiques. See the photograph below.

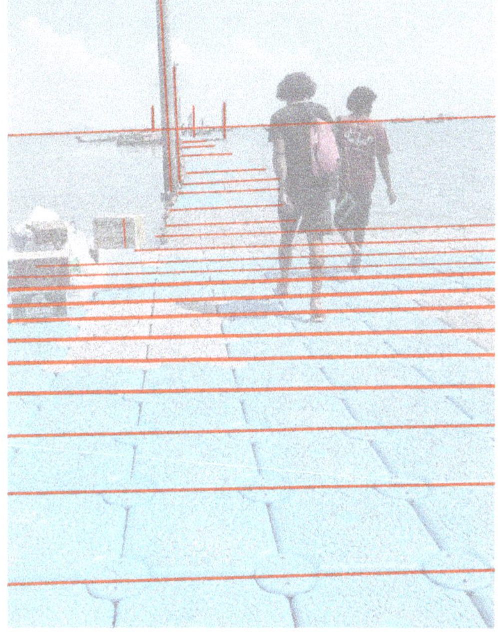

In the example below, there are areas of thick foliage, breaking the rhythm of the straight lines. The building on the left is at an odd angle, too.

The wires above are also not in alignment with the perspective lines.

See the picture on the below right to understand how the vanishing point and perspective lines are placed.

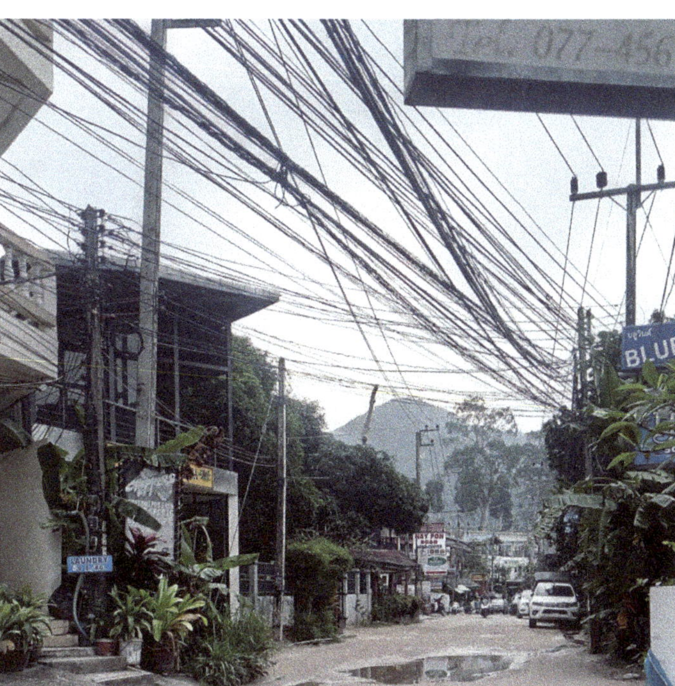

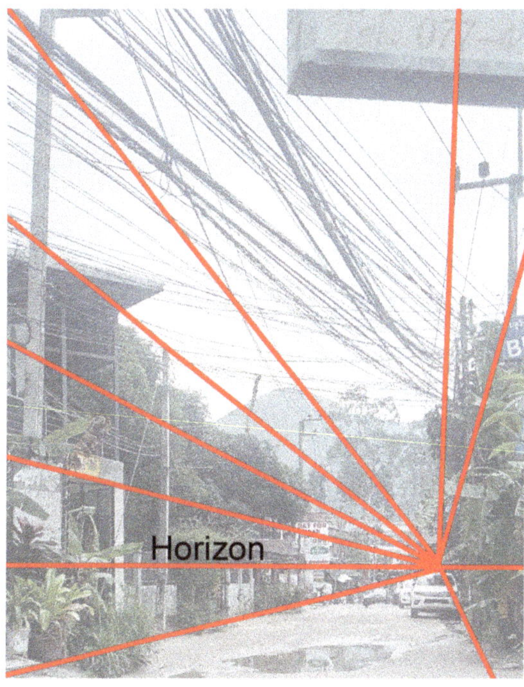

The best way to tackle foliage is as follows:

a) Draw the artificial shapes like poles and houses in line with the perspective lines. Keep white space for the foliage where it overlaps.

b) Block the rough shapes for trees and shrubs exactly as you see them. Don't worry about being in line with the perspective lines.

In the picture on the right, the foliage areas are marked with the diagonal lines.

First, finish drawing the artificial shapes. Then detail out the trees and shrubs as per their shapes marked earlier.

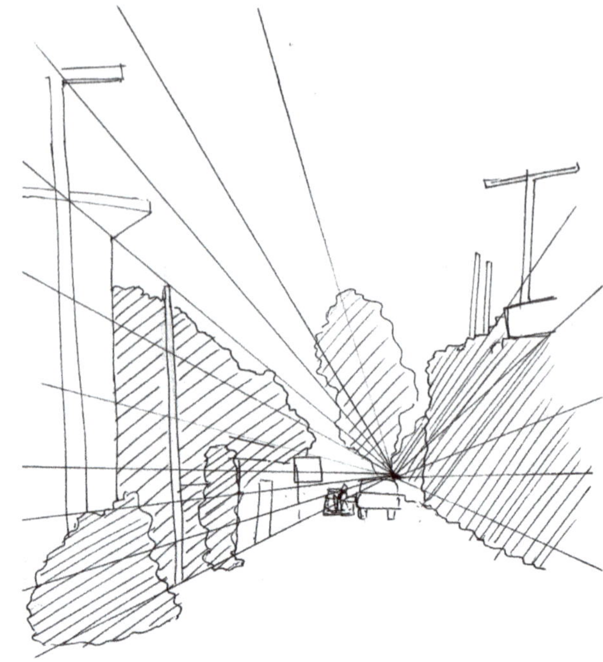

You may notice that the final sketch shown above is not exactly in line with the perspective lines. But as long as the sketch is sufficiently accurate, we are good.

Remember, the feel and aesthetics of the sketch are the most important. They should always take precedence over the pinpoint accuracy. Getting the perspective right is a means to an end, not the end itself.

Unless you are doing an architectural drawing!

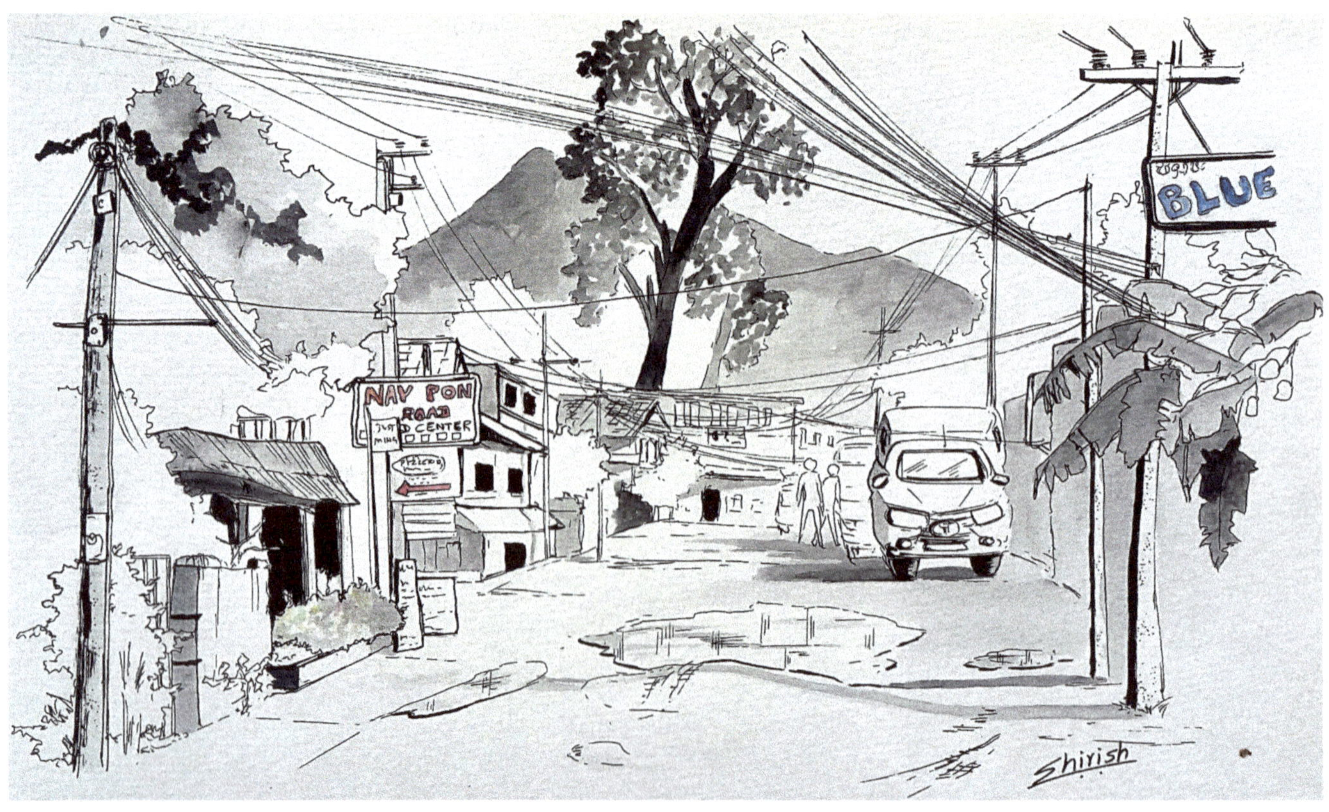

Here is a picture where the vanishing point is not so obvious.

The vanishing point is behind the tall tower at the center of the picture.

How did I come to know this?

Simple. I just drew perspective lines in line with the objects on the left and right. Where do you think they converged?

Yes, you guessed it correctly... the vanishing point!

The vanishing point is behind the tall tower at the center of the picture.

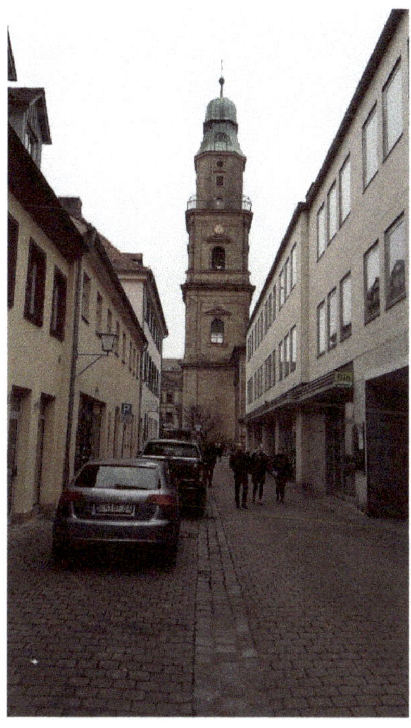

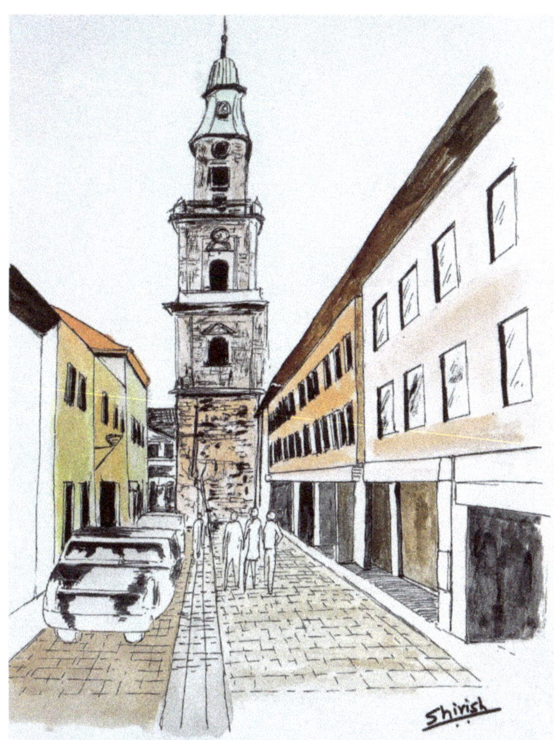

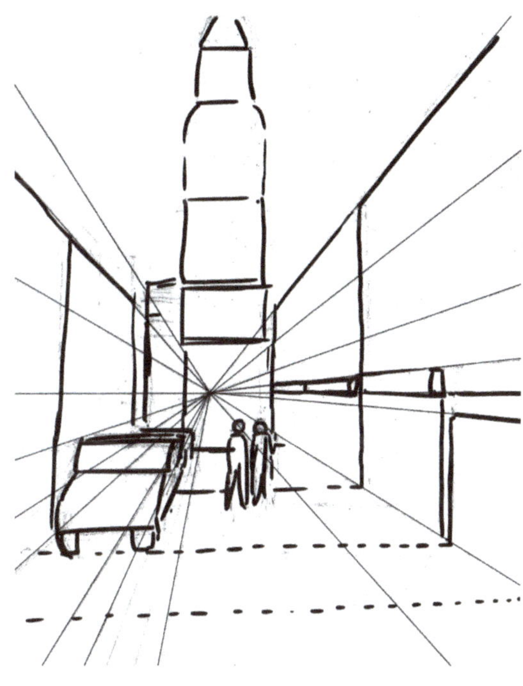

Bonus: Want to see how this picture was sketched? Head over to the following URL:

https://youtu.be/44nF3jB2l6I

(Alternatively, use the QR code given below) to watch the complete video of the making of this sketch. And don't forget to subscribe to the channel!

One point perspective (Pen, inks, watercolors)

Two-point Perspective

In two-point perspective, there are (obviously) two vanishing points. But you may also observe one more thing.

There are two planes visible as well.

As you can see in the picture on the right, two planes of the house are visible at the same time to us.

Two-point perspective has a similarity with one-point perspective.

Both the vanishing points are over the horizon line.

However, one, or even both the vanishing points may be outside the picture plane (i.e. the sketching paper/canvas). Note that I said, 'maybe'. It's not a necessity, though.

Both the planes always intersect each other forming a line.

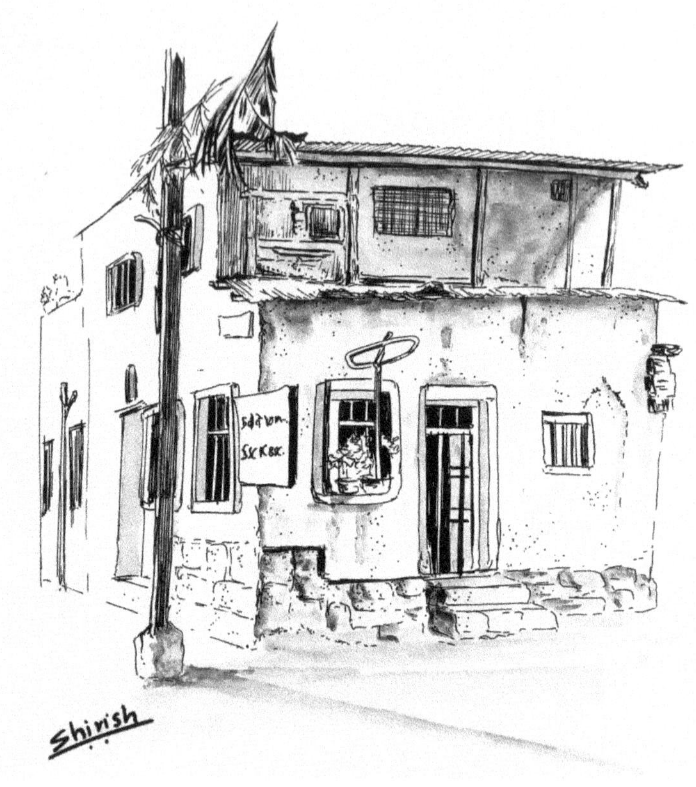

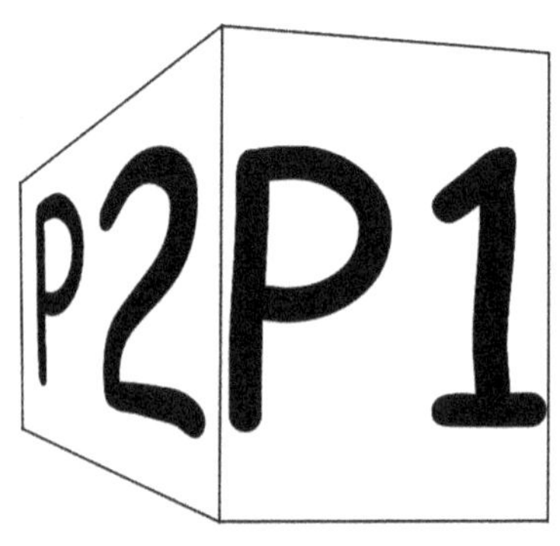

Below is an illustration of a two-point perspective, where one of the vanishing points is outside the picture plane.

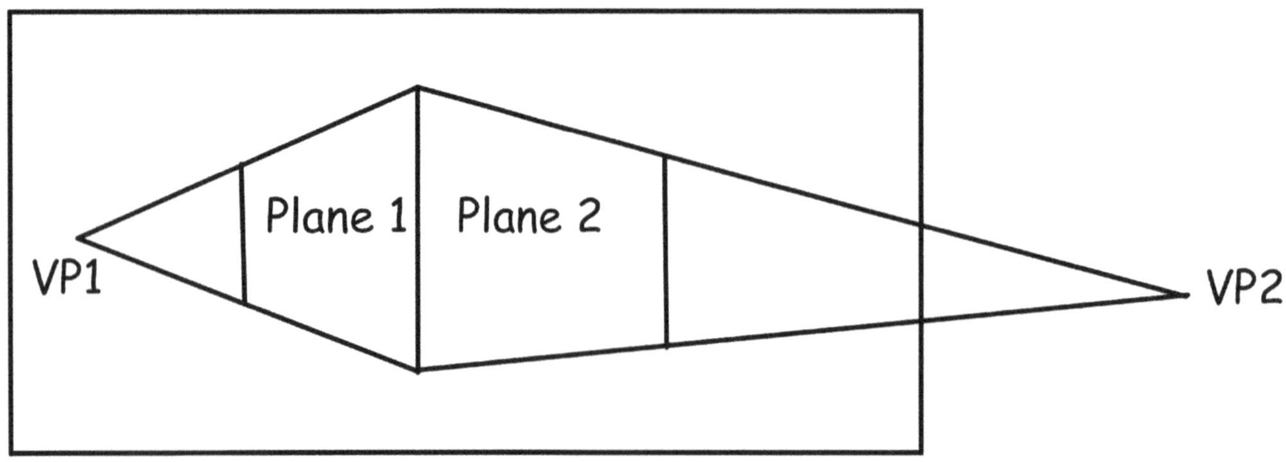

 Composition and Perspective

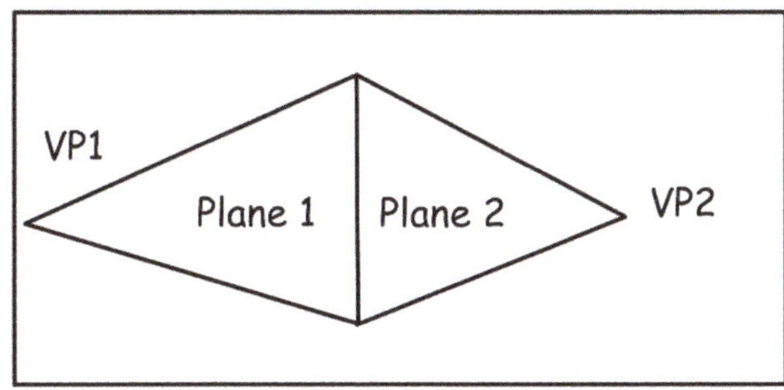

On the left is an illustration of a two-point perspective where both the vanishing points are inside the picture plane.

Below is an illustration of a two-point perspective where both the vanishing points are outside the picture plane.

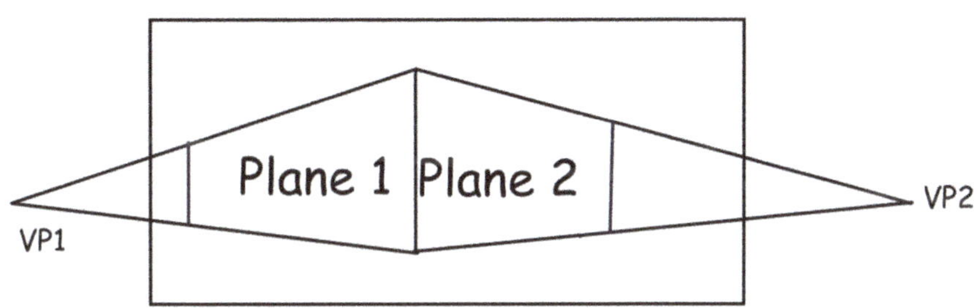

Let's see an example of drawing a two-point perspective sketch.

If the vanishing points are outside the paper, we may have to do some guesswork and draw the converging lines accordingly.

But you will not have to do any guesswork to complete the exercise below. Let's see how to draw this structure in two-point perspective.

You may observe that the right-side plane is steeper than the left plane.

We will ignore the overlapping shrub for the time being and focus solely on the structure.

The method which I will discuss now is the one I found the most useful. I don't claim that it's the only one, or the best one. However, let's see what this method is.

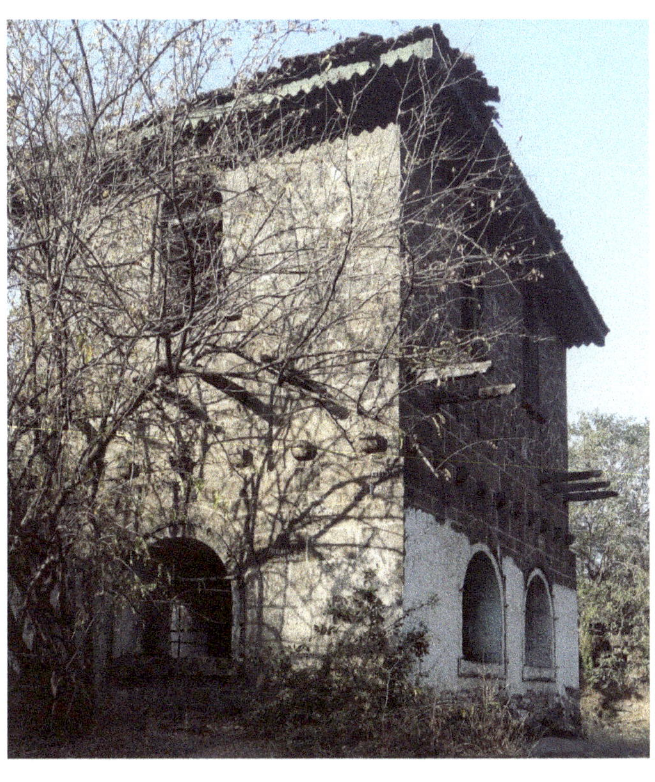

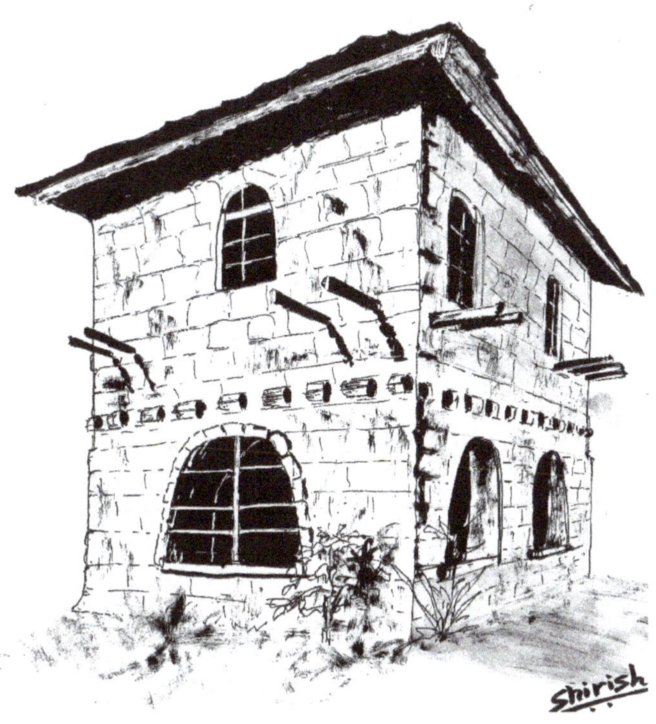

Let's start with identifying the intersection line of the plane and blocking the two planes. I found the vanishing point as shown on the right (pencil is pointing to the vanishing point). I held the paper firmly in place and extended the perspective lines such that they met outside the paper.

This was relatively easy for the right-side plane, which was steep.

Let's do the same for the left side plane.

Because the left side plane is less steep, the perspective lines extend way beyond the paper. The vanishing point is the small dot (marked with a circle) near the left end of the scale.

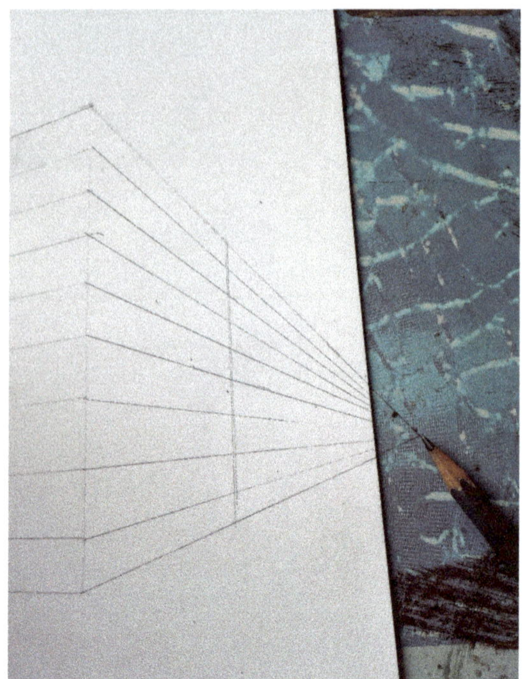

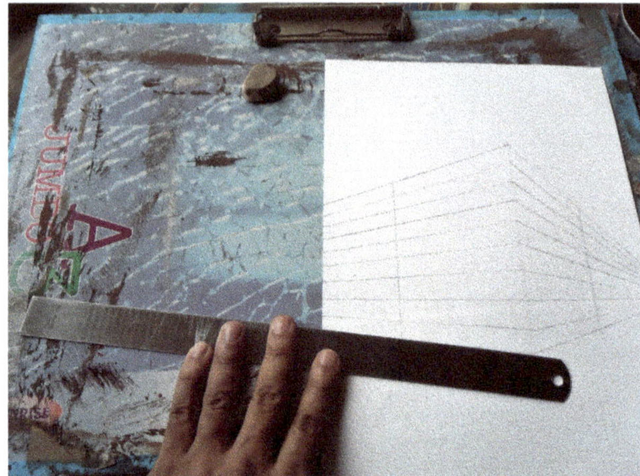

Bonus: Want to see how this picture was sketched? Head over to the following URL:

https://tinyurl.com/y7cb2dht

(Alternatively, use the QR code given below) to watch the complete video of the making of this sketch. And don't forget to subscribe to the channel!

Two point perspective

(Pen and black ink)

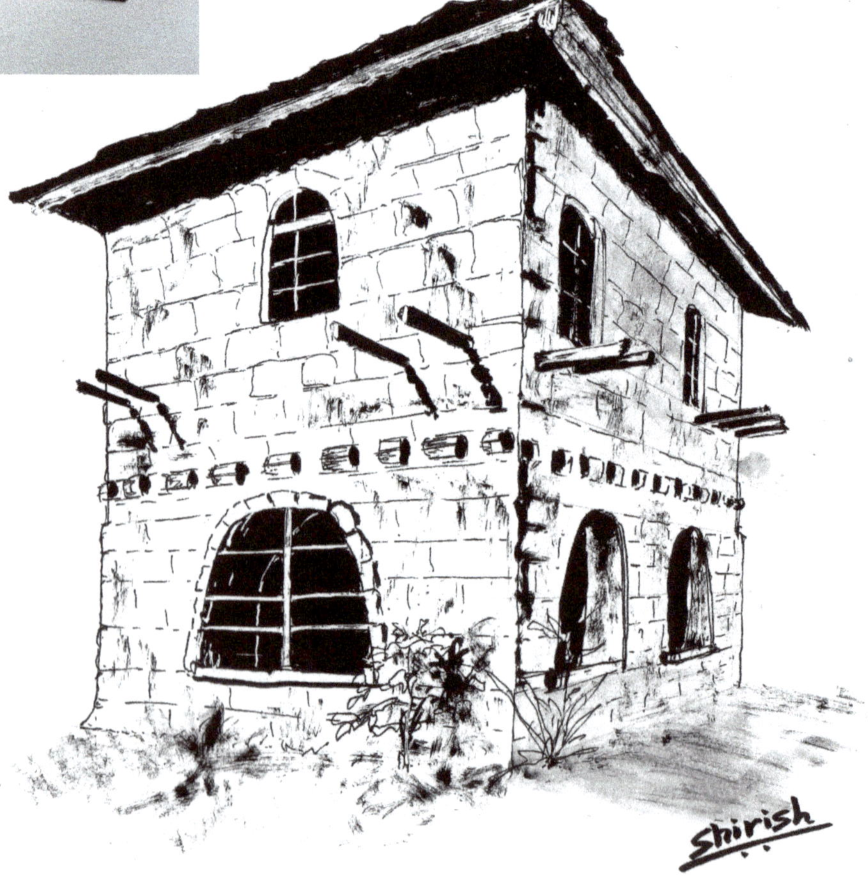

 Composition and Perspective

Three-point Perspective

Imagine yourself as a gravity-defying superhero flying over a bunch of skyscrapers. What do you see below?

Buildings?

Obviously!

But how do you see these buildings?

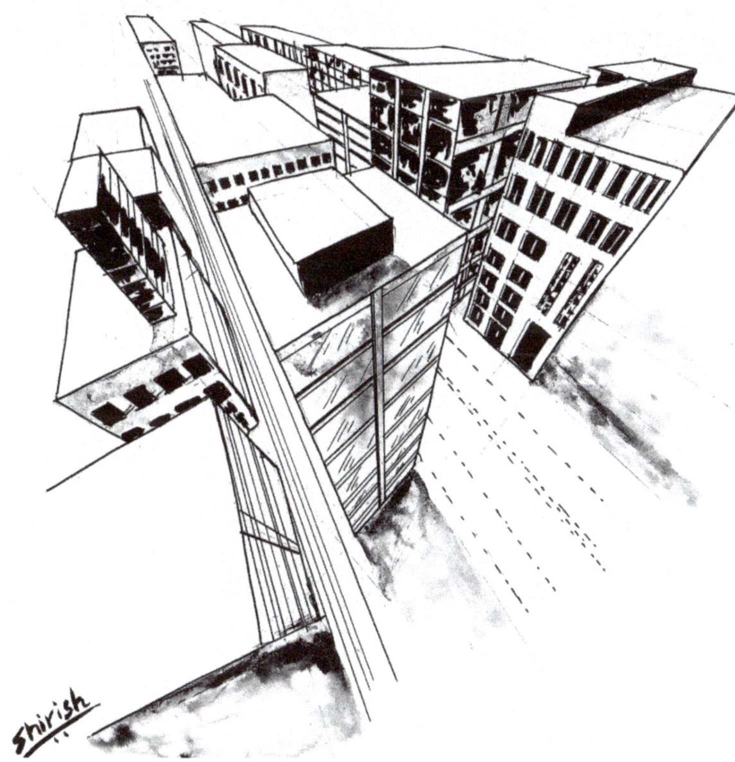

You can see their tops, as well as two sides.

In other words, you can see the two sides (planes) of any building (like in two-point perspective), AND the top of the building (third plane).

Bonus: Want to see how this picture was sketched? Head over to the following URL:

https://tinyurl.com/y7qlcckp

(Alternatively, use the QR code given below) to watch the complete video of the making of this sketch. And don't forget to subscribe to the channel!

Three-point perspective

(Pen and black ink)

Three-point perspective is most evident when we look at an element from below (worm's eye view) or above (bird's eye view).

So where are the vanishing points, and where is the horizon?

Aha!

This is where three-point perspective is radically different from one and two-point perspectives.

In three-point perspective, there's not one, not two, but three horizons. Every horizon intersects the other two at a vanishing point each.

And three vanishing points, in three corners of the picture.

Every horizon passes through two vanishing points.

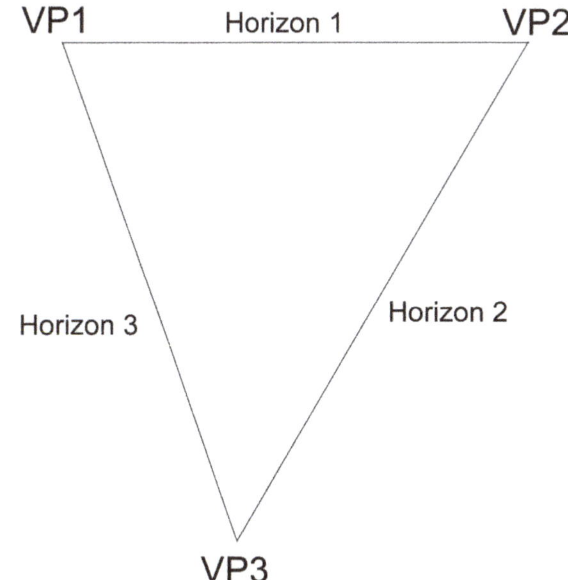

In one-point perspective, there's one picture plane (facing the viewer).

In two-point perspective, there are two picture planes (intersecting in front of the viewer).

In three-point perspective, there's a picture cube!

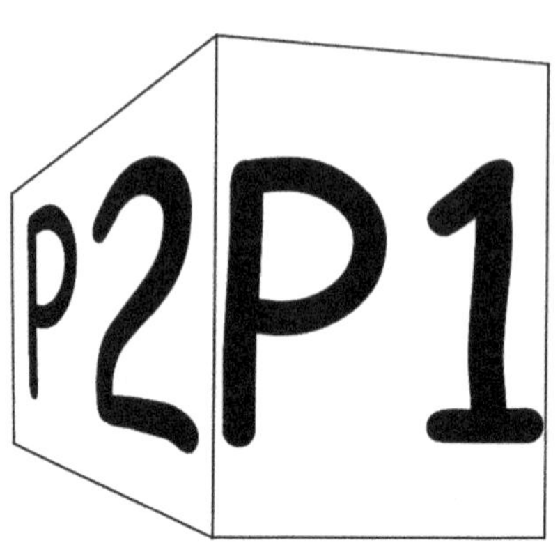

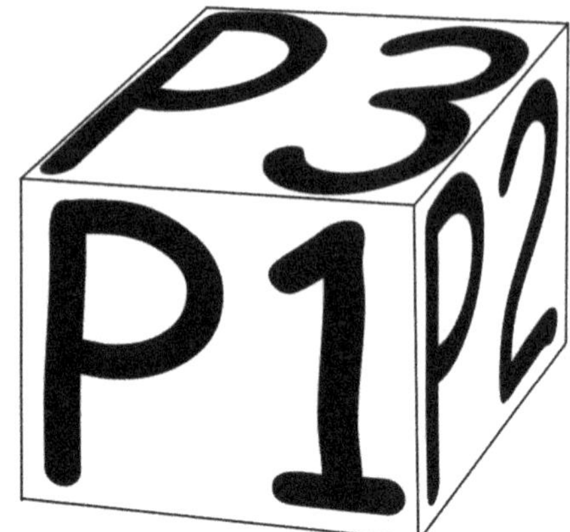

Just like two-point perspective, one or more vanishing points may be outside the paper.

Now let's do a bird's eye view sketch using the three-point perspective. For the sake of simplicity, we will keep all the three vanishing points within the picture plane.

There's a side effect of having all the three vanishing points within the picture plane. The perspective becomes somewhat 'extreme' (think vertigo effect). The buildings will appear as if we are floating right over the edge of these buildings.

The picture on the right is an example of the extreme three-point perspective (bird's eye view).

Here, not only all the vanishing points are within the picture plane, but the ground level is the same as the lower vanishing point. So, the lower edges of all the buildings converge into a single point.

There's no need to have such an extreme perspective all the time, though. Refer to the picture at the beginning of this chapter on the three-point perspective. You will notice that the bases of the buildings are well above the vanishing point.

In fact, the three-point perspective drawings need not be extreme at all. Look at the picture on the next page to see what I mean.

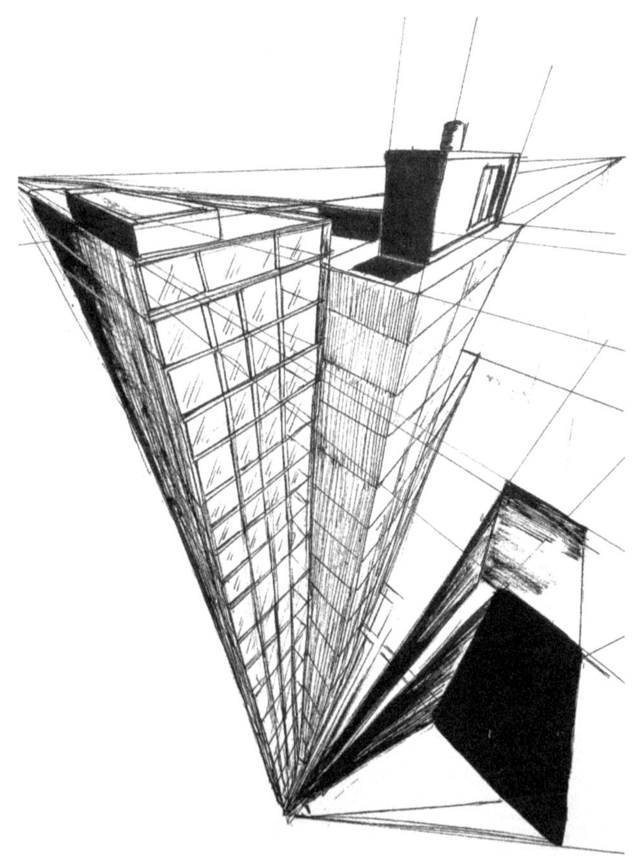

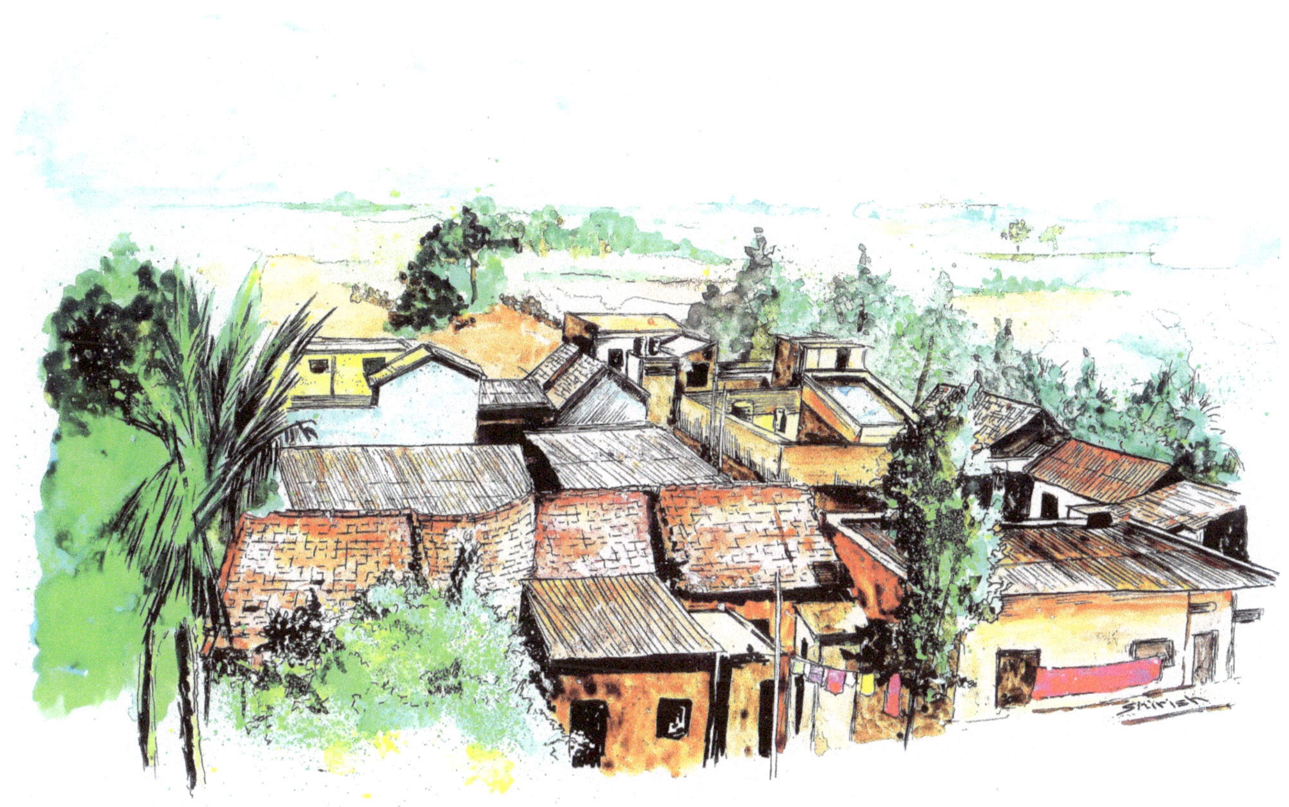

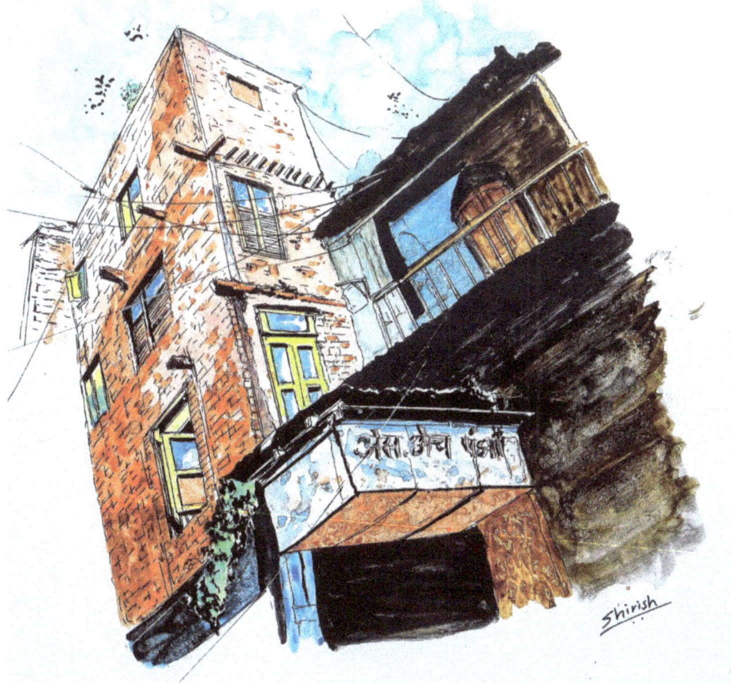

Three-point perspective can also be drawn in a worm's eye view mode. In this case, we are looking at an object looking up. The principles remain the same. The only difference is that one of the vanishing points is present towards the sky.

Here's an example of a worm's eye view perspective sketch.

Bonus: Want to see how this picture was sketched? Head over to the following URL:

https://tinyurl.com/yb9bszpl

(Alternatively, use the QR code given below) to watch the complete video of the making of this sketch. And don't forget to subscribe to the channel!

Three-point perspective (worm's eye view)

(Pen, inks, watercolors)

Now let's learn how to draw a three-point perspective drawing. We will draw several buildings in this bird's eye view perspective sketch.

You will need a piece of paper, a ruler, a pencil and an eraser for this drawing.

First, mark 3 points and join them with each other as shown here.

I have also shown the edge of the paper to give you an idea of how to position the vanishing points.

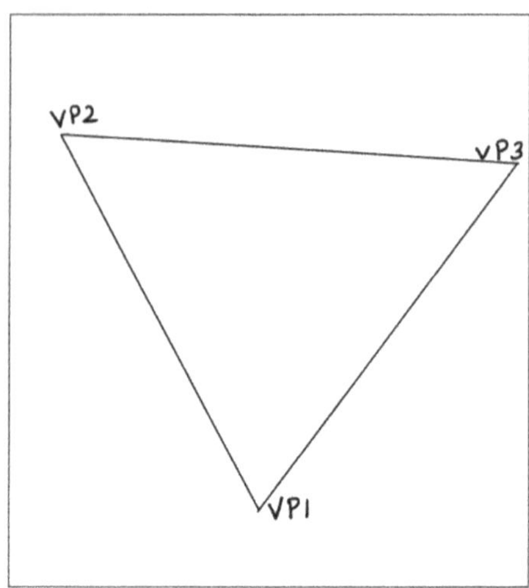

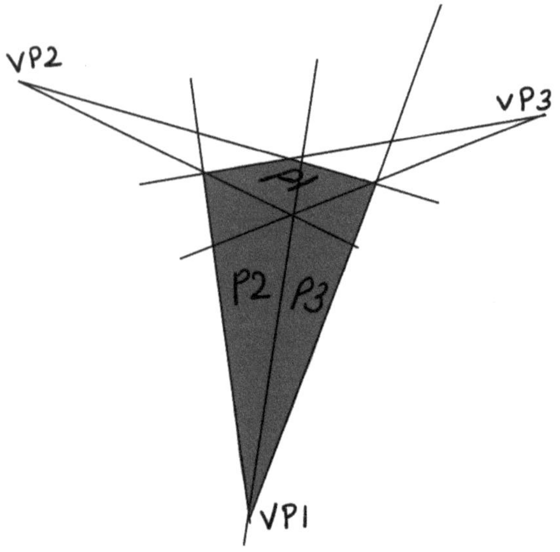

The picture on the left will give you an idea of how the planes will be formed in the drawing. Each plane is formed by lines originating from two vanishing points at a time.

Plane P1 is formed by lines originating from VP2 and VP3.

Plane P2 is formed by lines originating from VP1 and VP2.

Plane P3 is formed by lines originating from VP1 and VP3.

We will start with the upper planes. Start drawing perspective lines from VP2 and VP3 and let them intersect to form the tops of the buildings.

In the drawing on the right, I have marked the tops of a few buildings in dark shades.

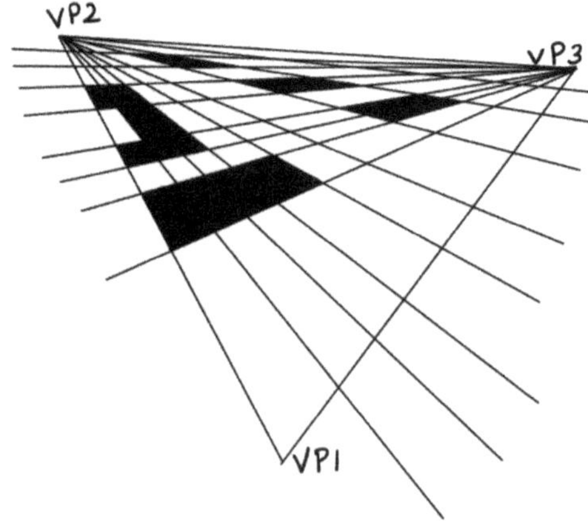

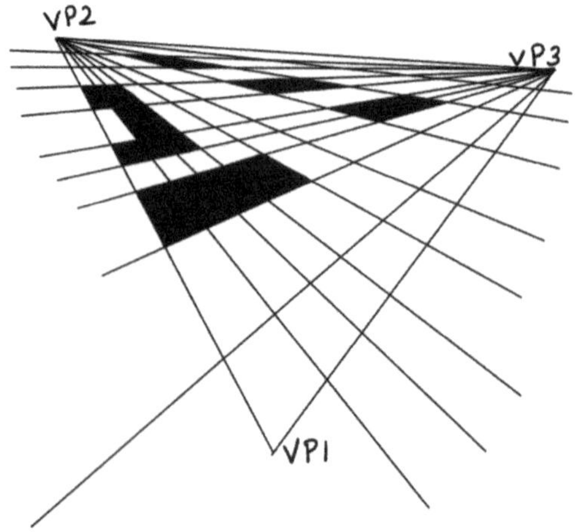

Now let's draw one line from VP3 intersecting the horizon between VP1 and VP2 (left). This line will mark the ground level for our buildings.

I have drawn this line extra-long to differentiate it from the rest.

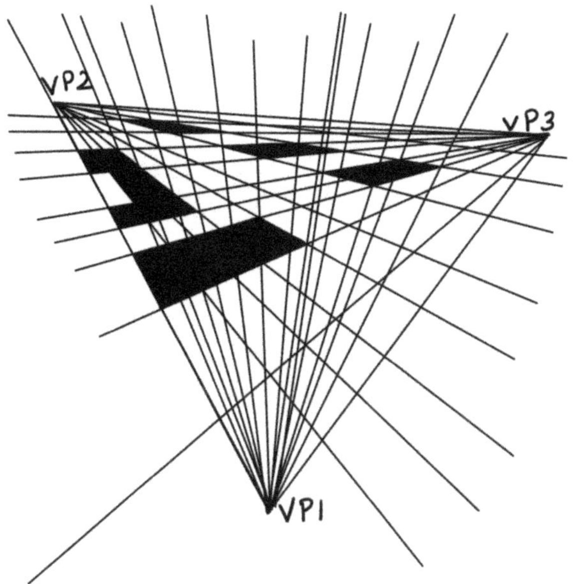

Let's draw lines from VP1 to form rest of the two planes for the buildings.

Make sure these lines pass through all the vertices of each of the building tops.

Now we simply need to shade the plane formed by the intersecting lines between VP1 and VP3. Restrict the shading to the ground level line.

Now let's identify the third plane, which is formed by the intersecting lines from VP1 and VP2.

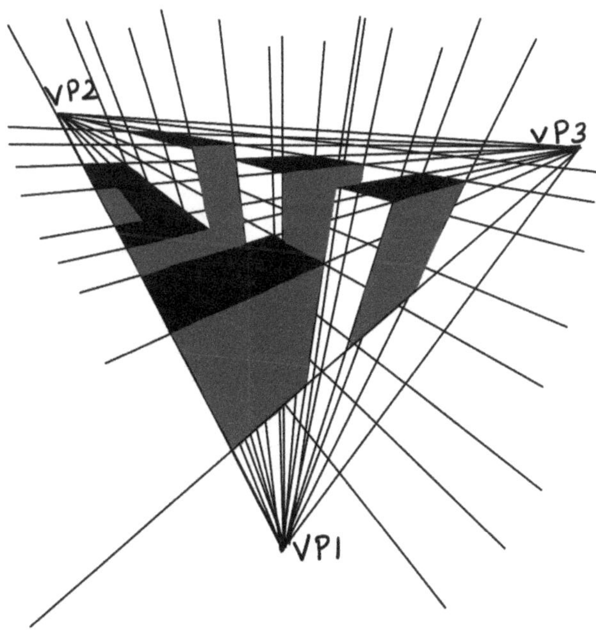

And, we already have the basic structure of our buildings ready. To add details (windows etc.) to those buildings, simply repeat the following steps:

- Choose the plane on which you want to draw the details.

- Find out the vanishing points which contribute to this plane.

- Draw intersecting perspective lines from these two vanishing points. Keep the details confined to those lines.

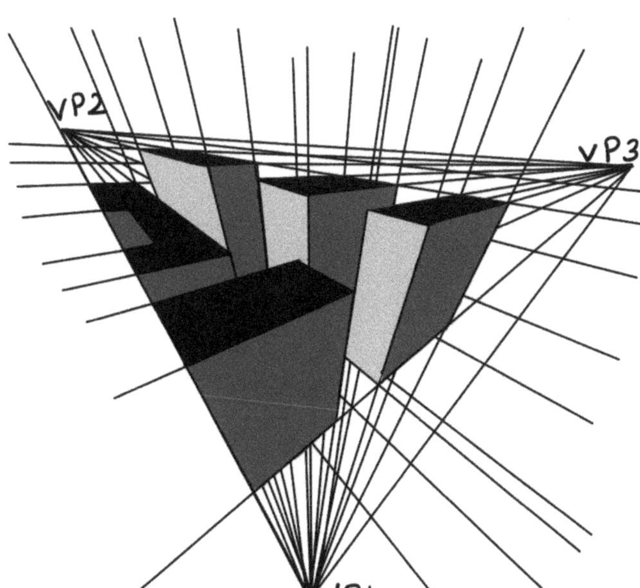

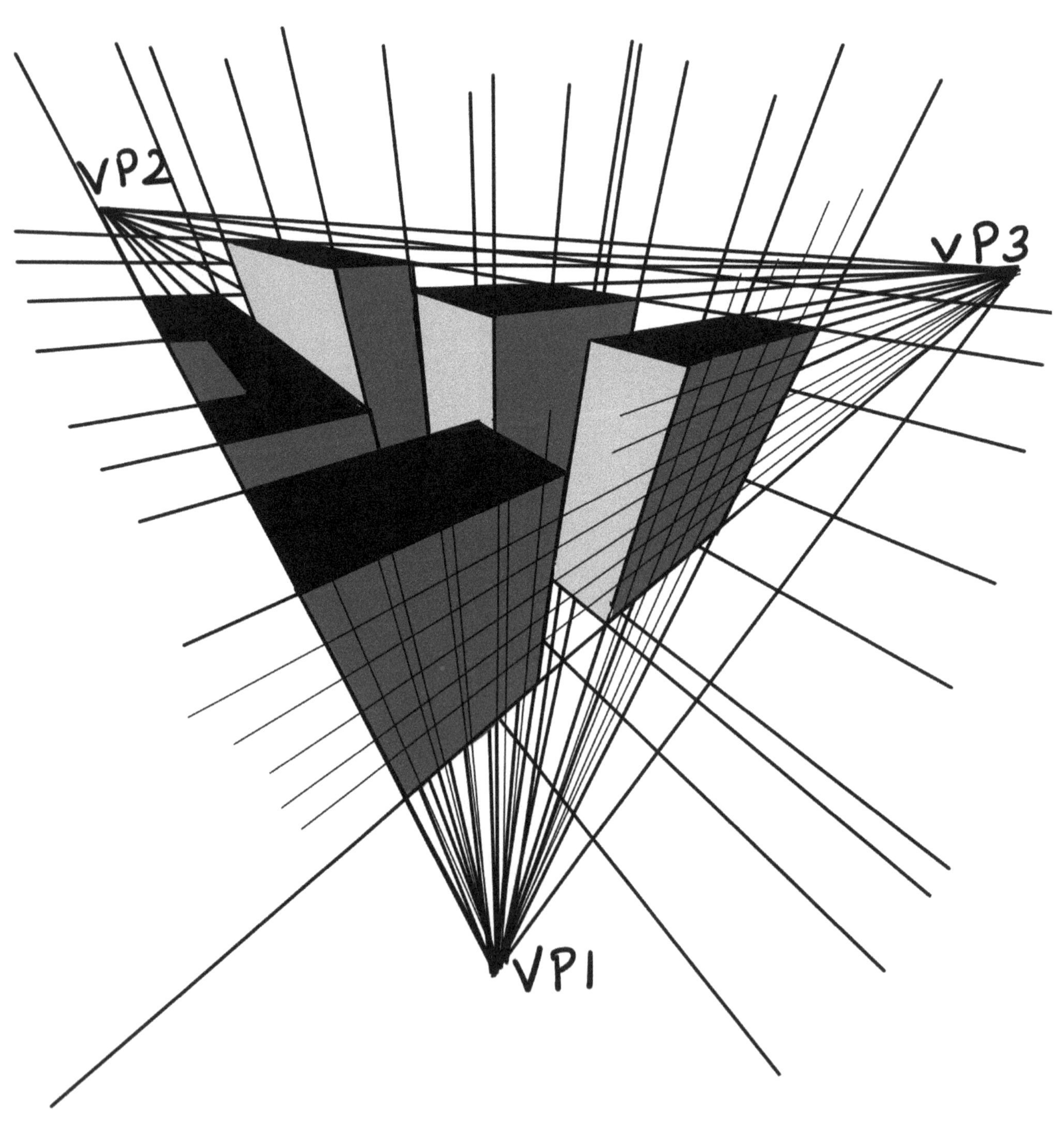

VP2
VP3
VP1

Five-point (Fisheye) Perspective

This is one of the more 'exotic' perspective types.

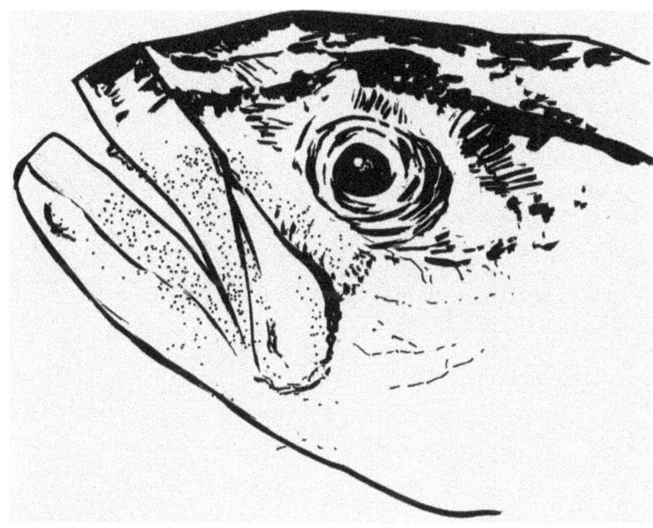

Even more exotic than vertigo-inducing three-point perspective!

There's one more name for this perspective.

The Fisheye Perspective.

Pretty self-explanatory, huh?

No? Ok, let me enlighten you.

If you look a fish in the eye, you can see that the fisheye is bulgy.

It acts like a convex surface or a very wide-angle lens.

In plain English, it means that the fisheye covers more area at a time than a human eye can see (close to 180 degrees view).

Is there any downside to this super-ability?

Sure, there is. How is a super-ability possible without any downside? It would be too good to be true, right?

So… here it is.

When covering such a large area with the convex lens, the whole picture appears distorted. Things appear quite different from how they are.

But isn't that the whole point of learning perspective? To understand the way, we see things and the way things are?

Believe me, things appear much, much different than they are from a fish's perspective.

Let's see how.

Below on the left is a picture of a 'normal' building in two-point (human eye) perspective. On the right is the picture of the same building in five-point perspective.

You can see how the objects in the picture appear more and more distorted as we move towards the edges? You may also see that the central part of the object is relatively less distorted, but it's still curving out.

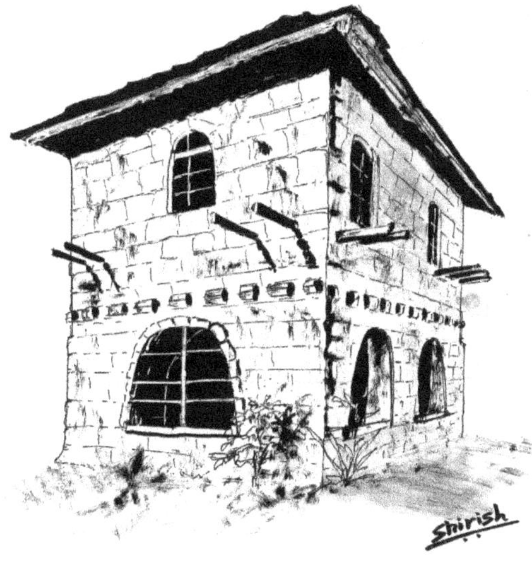

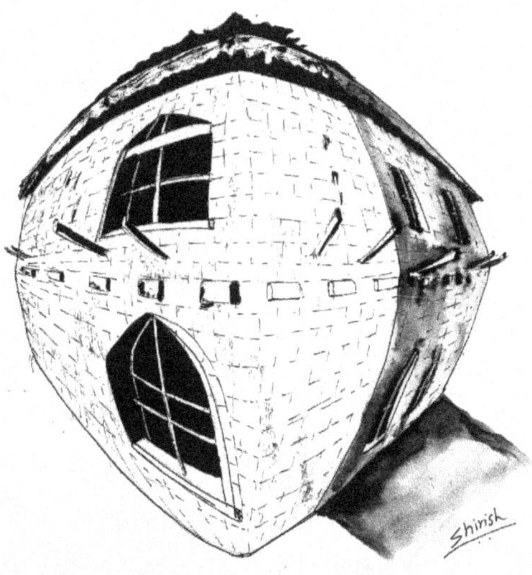

Let's see how to draw a picture in five-point perspective.

Let's begin drawing a five-point perspective sketch. Start with an oval intersected by 2 lines as shown below.

The five points where the two lines intersect each other, and the oval are the five vanishing points.

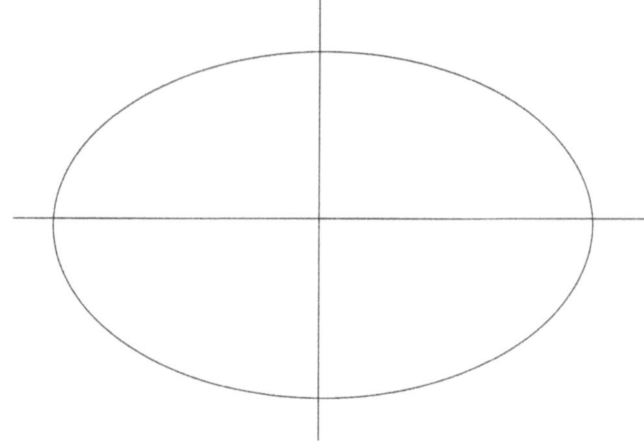

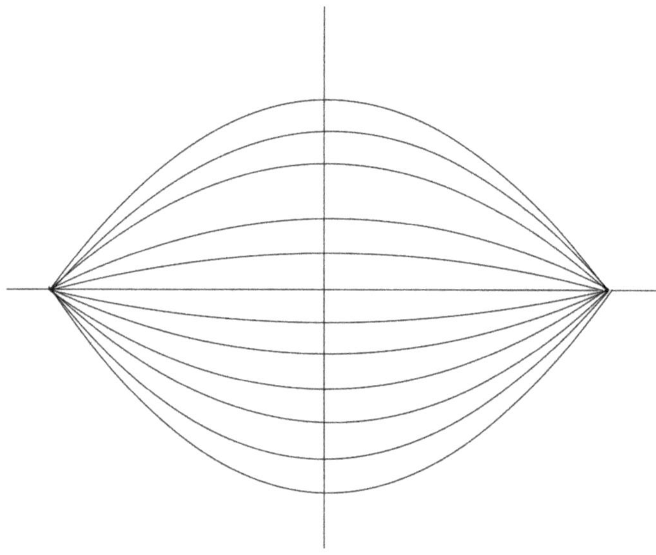

Draw curved lines as shown here, from left to right. This is our first set of the perspective lines.

Now do the same from top to bottom to get another set of perspective line.

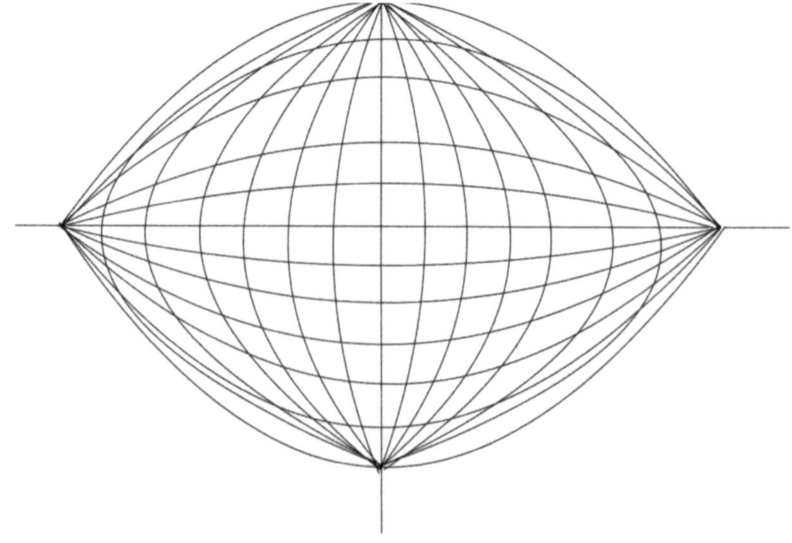

Composition and Perspective

We can use these perspective lines to come up with the left and right planes of the buildings as shown below:

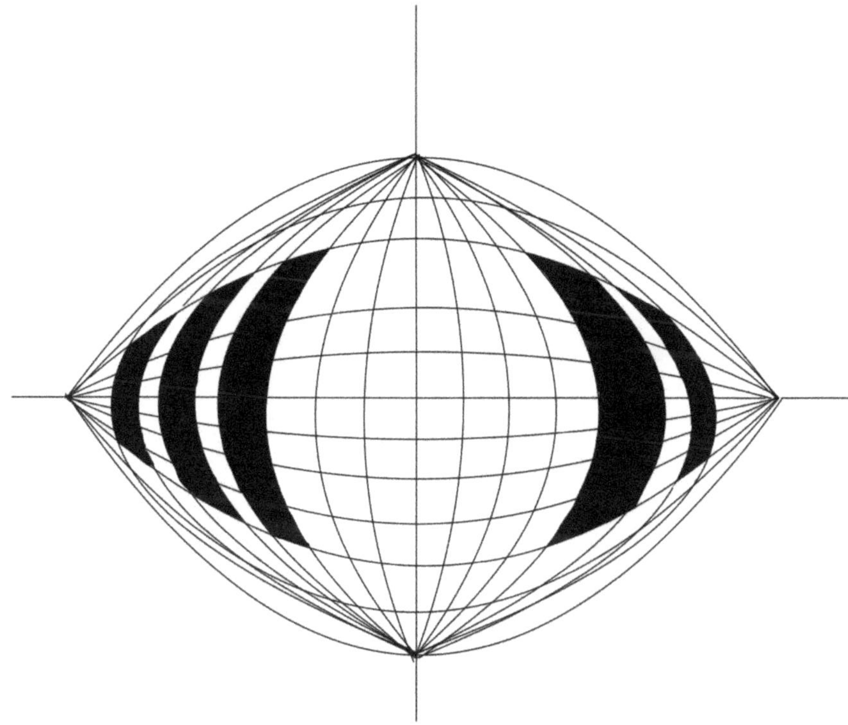

Draw radiating lines connecting the central vanishing point with the vertices of these planes.

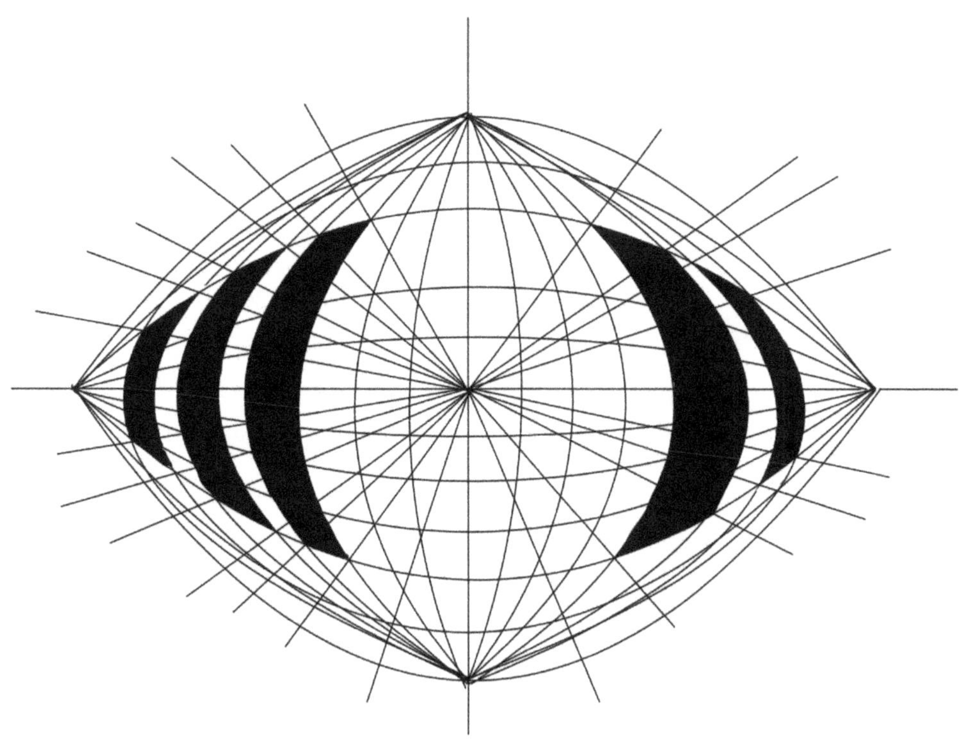

These outward radiating lines will translate into the inner planes of the buildings as shown below. Note how the building in the middle of the picture looks slightly curvy but has the least distortion.

As we go away from the center towards the edges, the picture gets more and more distorted.

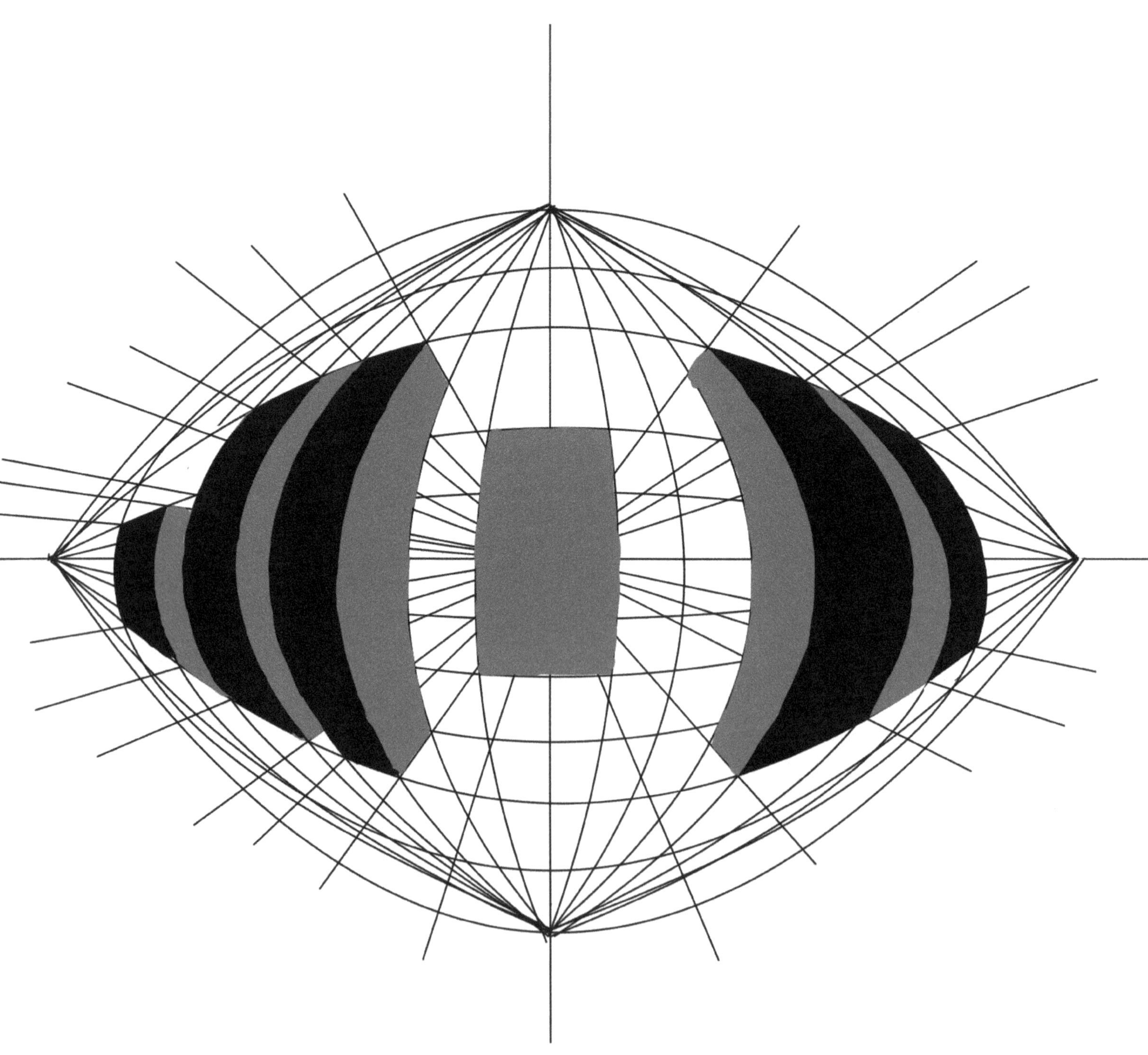

Composition and Perspective

Another interesting fact:

Imagine that you are standing at the top of a neighboring building.

This building is of half the height as our target building. Also, you are looking at this building at an angle.

How will you see the target building?

You will see its side plane, as well as the front side. You will also see the target building extending upward and downward at the same time. This will create a four-point perspective!

The following pictures show some examples of five-point perspective.

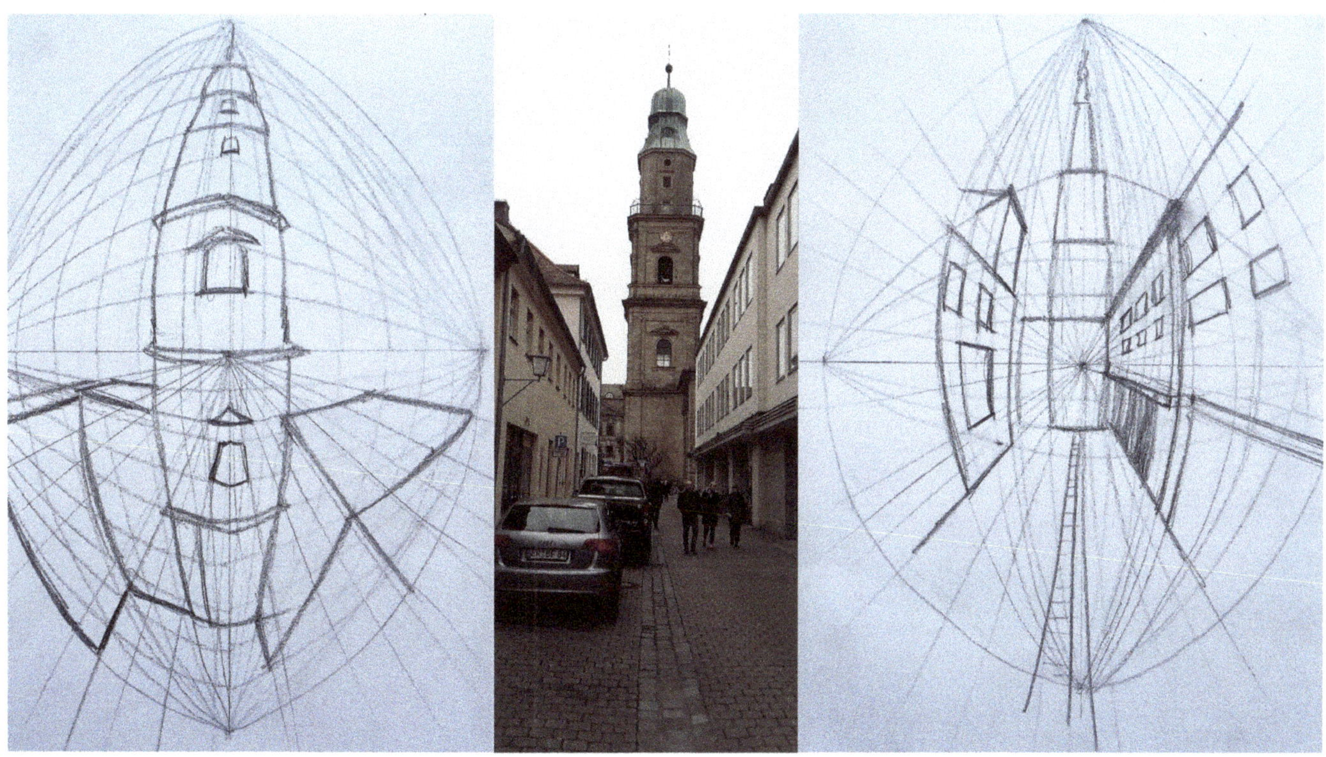

Bonus: Want to see how the picture on the previous page was sketched? Head over to the following links (or QR code) given below to watch the complete video of the making of this sketch. And don't forget to subscribe to the channel!

Part 1: https://youtu.be/U8wwztLY9YI

Part 2: https://youtu.be/GlXmQnSEXcA

Five-point perspective – Part 1 and 2 (Pencils)

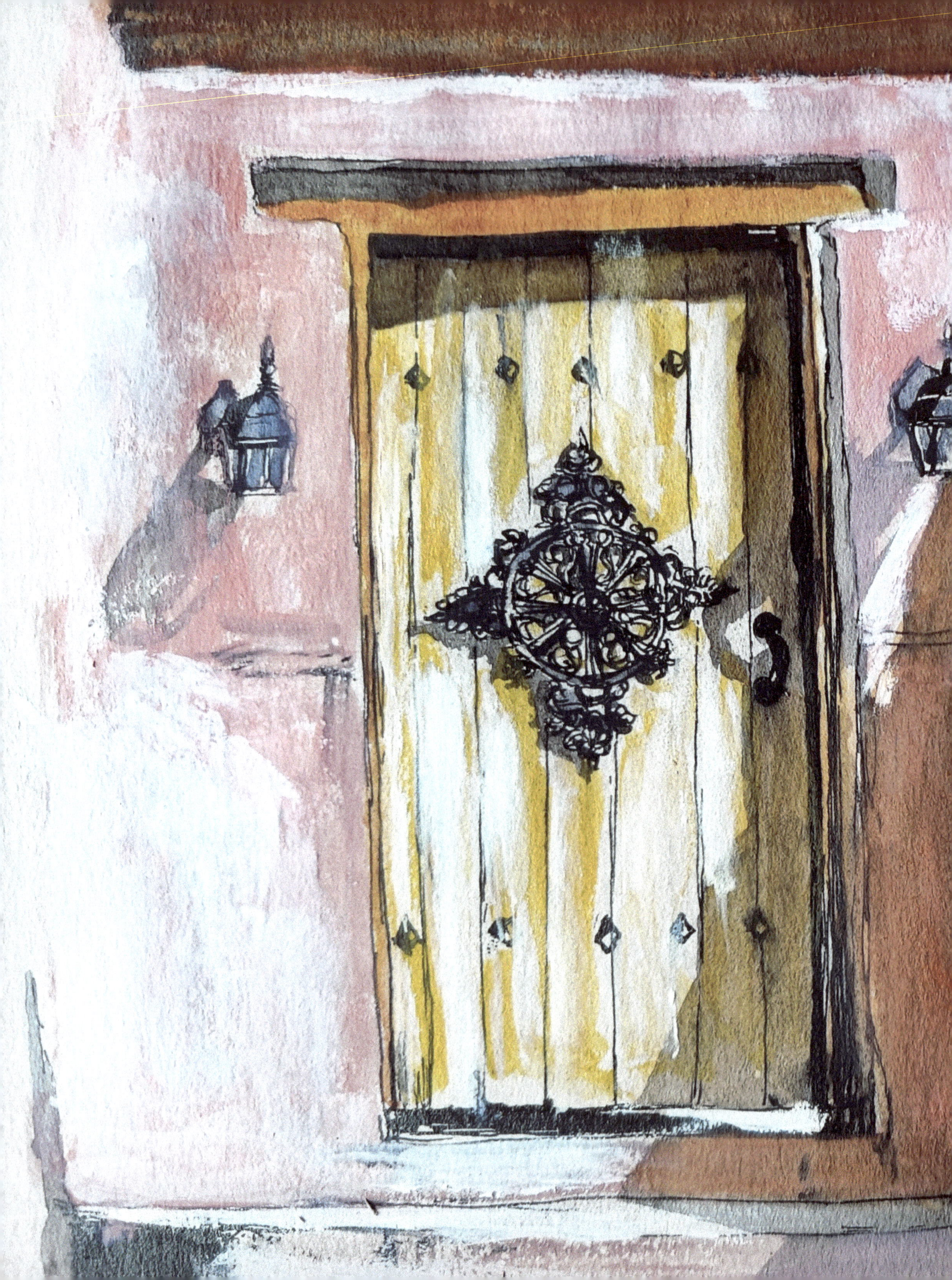

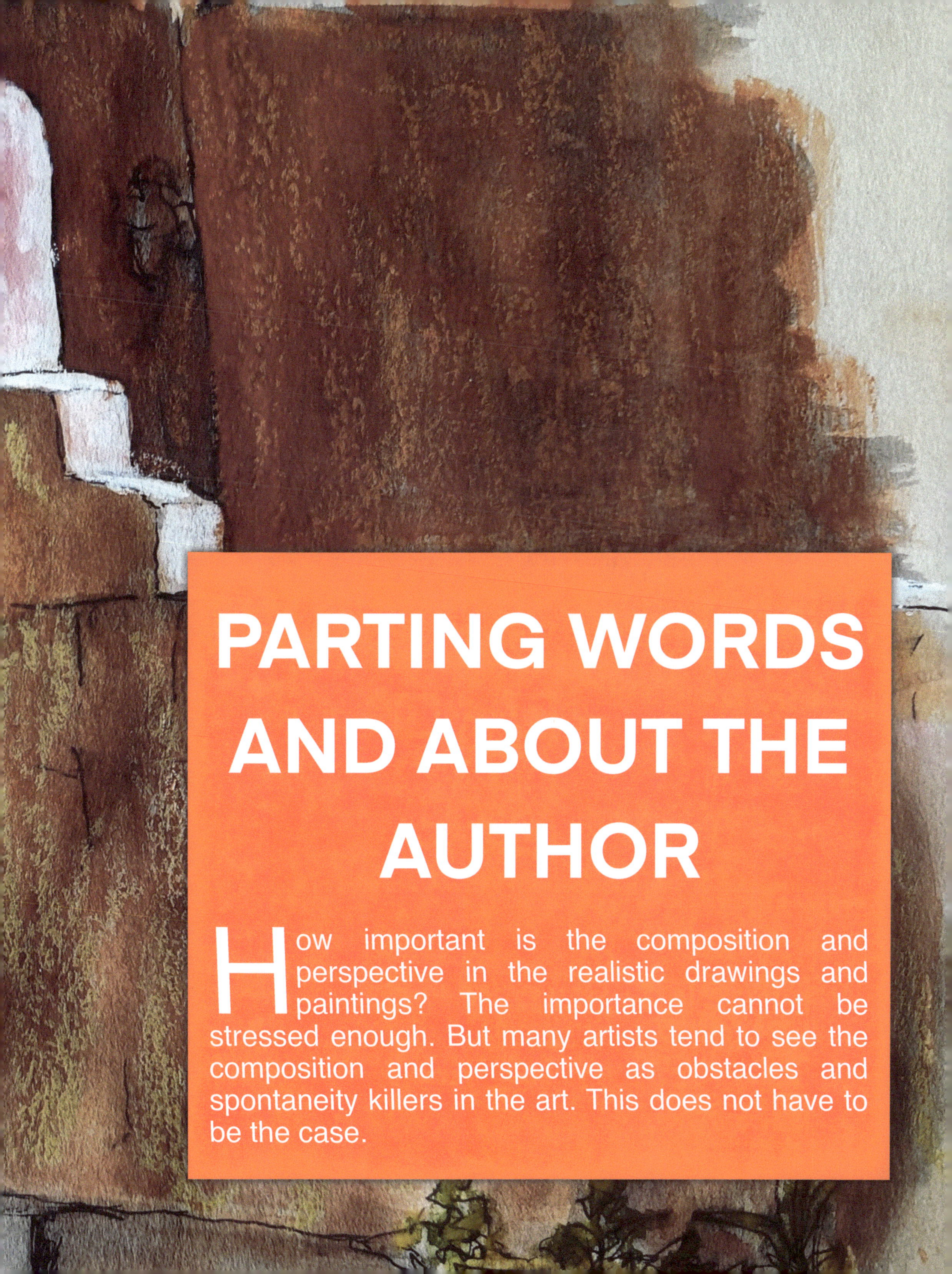

PARTING WORDS AND ABOUT THE AUTHOR

How important is the composition and perspective in the realistic drawings and paintings? The importance cannot be stressed enough. But many artists tend to see the composition and perspective as obstacles and spontaneity killers in the art. This does not have to be the case.

I hope that through this book I have given you a new perspective to look at the perspective (pun intended), as an ally, rather than an adversary.

So let's go out there and look at the world from a whole new perspective!

Happy sketching :-)

Ohh… and did I mention my website?

And my YouTube channel?

And my video courses?

And other books of mine on the very subject of sketching?

Keep reading to get to know about all about these.

About Shirish:

Shirish is a self-taught artist based in a very populous city called Pune, in a very populous country Shirish is a self-taught artist based in a very populous city called Pune, in a very populous country called India.

Shirish has worked in the thriving IT Industry for more than two decades. But he is an artist by heart. Sketching, painting and teaching art is Shirish's first, second and third love (not necessarily in that sequence!).

Shirish dabbles in various subjects such as landscapes, portraits, figure studies and abstracts. He works in various media like Pen & Inks, Watercolors, Oils, Acrylics, Spray Paints, and Digital art.

Shirish has participated in many art exhibitions, and his sketches and paintings are present in private collections in India and various other countries.

Shirish has published some very successful video courses on various online platforms, which he produces himself. These courses have helped thousands of students worldwide learn the intricacies of sketching and painting.

Shirish is the author of various bestselling art instruction books.

https://www.huesandtones.net/books/

If you want regular updates and free goodies from me, consider subscribing to my mailing list. I never share your email ID with anyone because I hate spam as much as you do.

https://HuesAndTones.net/signup/

But I do believe in sharing a lot of quality content with my readers and offering them discounts. When you subscribe to my mailing list, you will get a printable PDF of my adult colouring book 'Dystopian Encounters' as well as some more free goodies.

You can get access of a host of free training materials and videos on my website. You can also check out my other books (available in multiple languages) on my website. All of my social media links are also given on the next couple of pages.

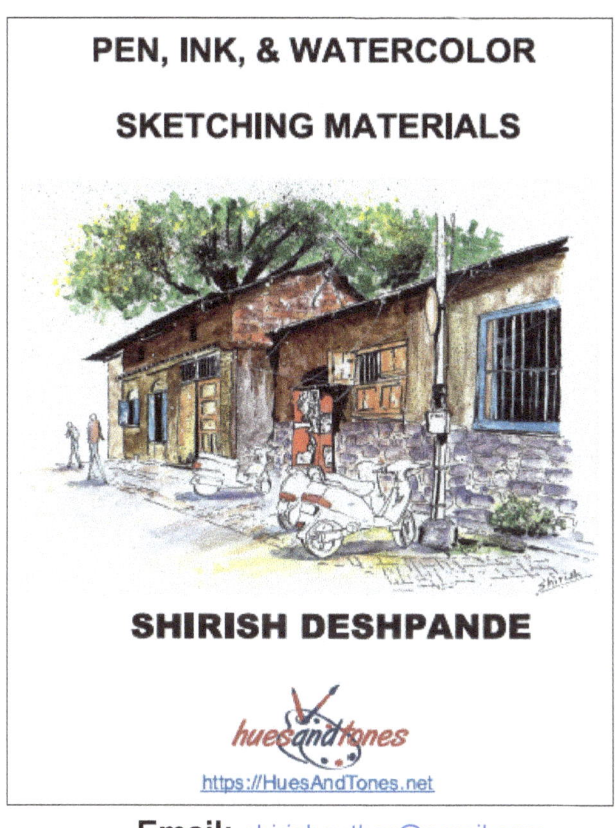

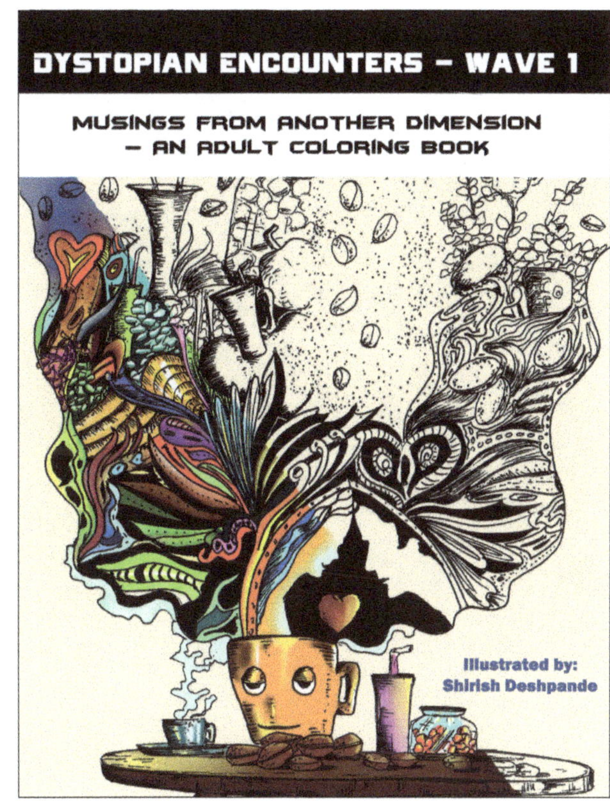

Email: shirishauthor@gmail.com

Website: https://HuesAndTones.net/

YouTube:
https://Youtube.com/c/huesandtones/

Video Trainings:
https://HuesAndTones.net/courses/

Gratitude

I am extremely grateful to my wife Aparna. She has consistently stood with me, encouraged me and tolerated me through all my artistic endeavors and eccentricities.

I am thankful to the many fellow artists, authors, and creatives, who keep inspiring me every day. You guys are awesome!

Happy Sketching :-)

Request for Review

Did you receive any value from this book? Did you enjoy reading it?

If yes, would you please leave a review at the store you bought the book from?

Your review will help the book reach more readers worldwide and help them learn to sketch like a boss.

After all, the joy multiplies when shared, right? :-)

Also by Shirish (Ebook, Paperback, Hardcover)

https://HuesAndTones.net/books/

For the beginner and intermediate artists who want to explore sketching with pen and ink

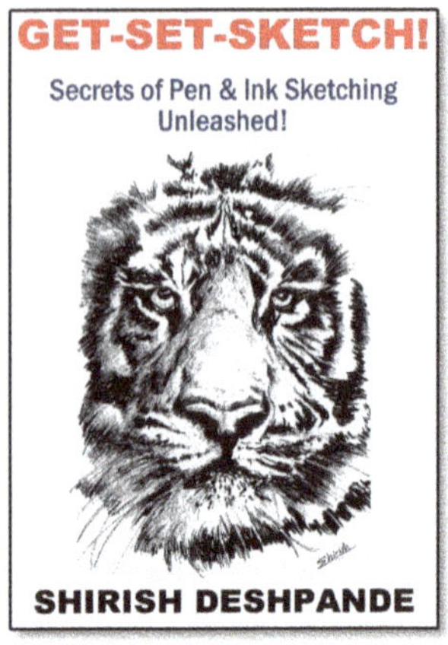

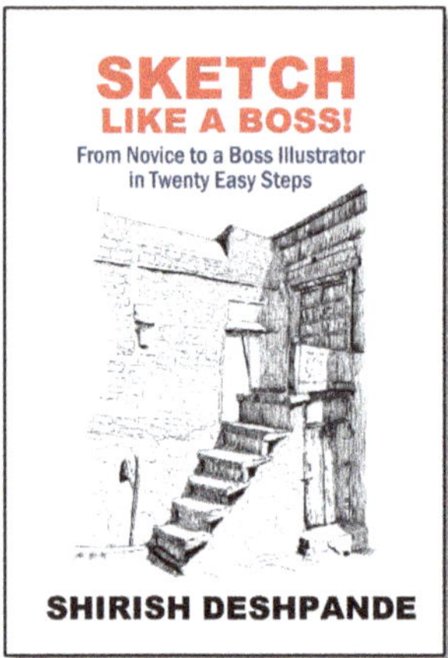

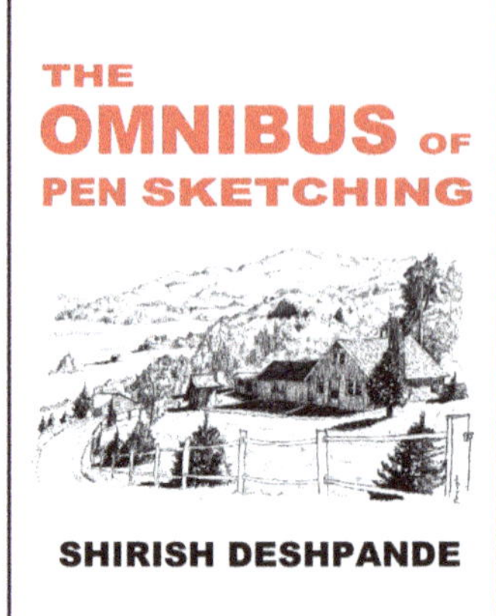

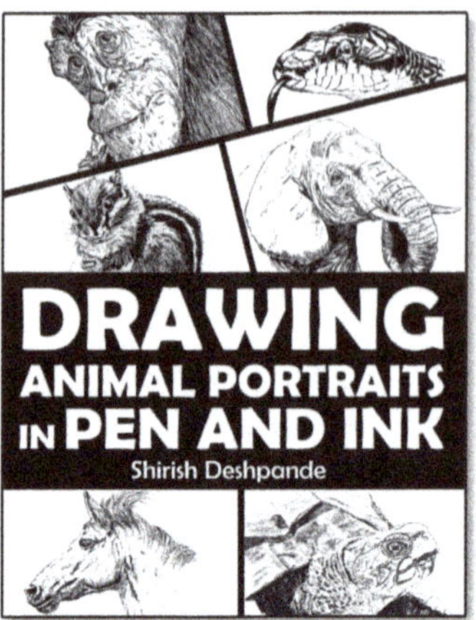

For the artists who want to move into the colorful world of watercolor painting

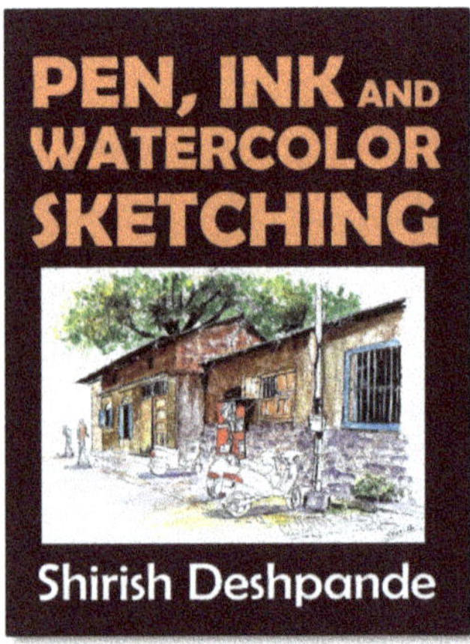

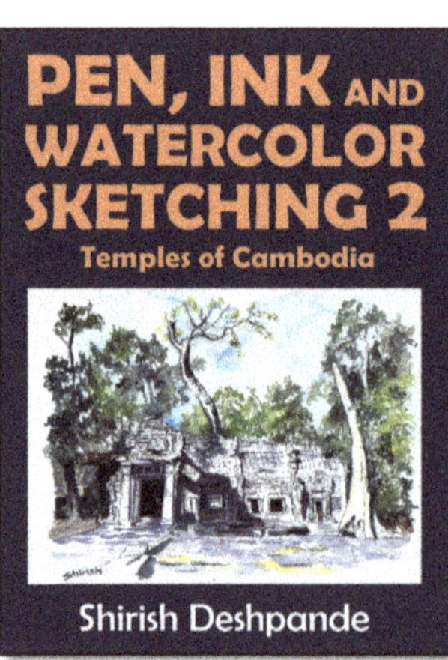

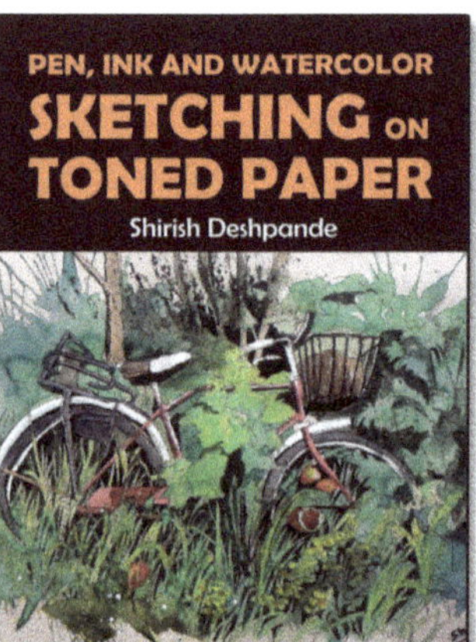

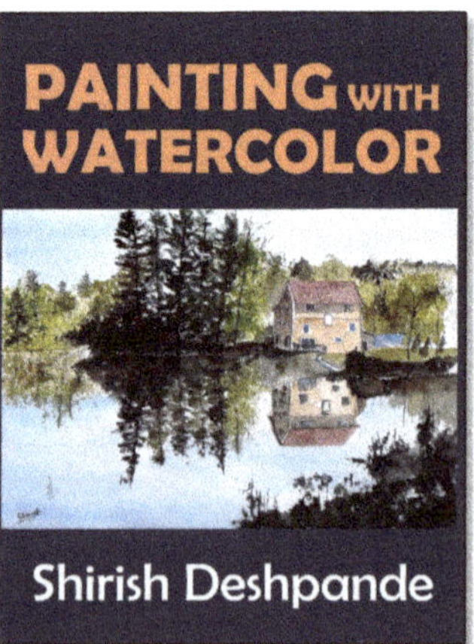

For the artists who are not afraid to experiment with various mediums and subjects

For the artists who want to paint expressively using digital medium

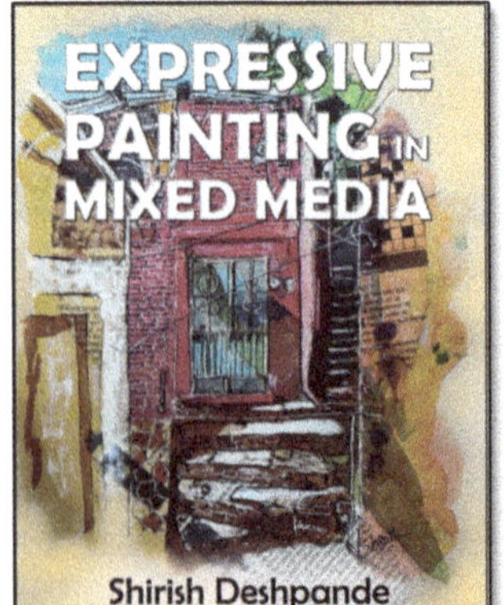

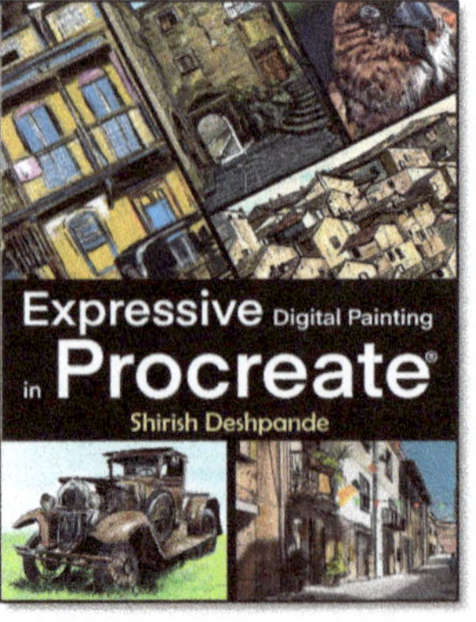

Composition and Perspective

Box sets (book bundles)

https://huesandtones.net/collections/book-bundles

EBooks

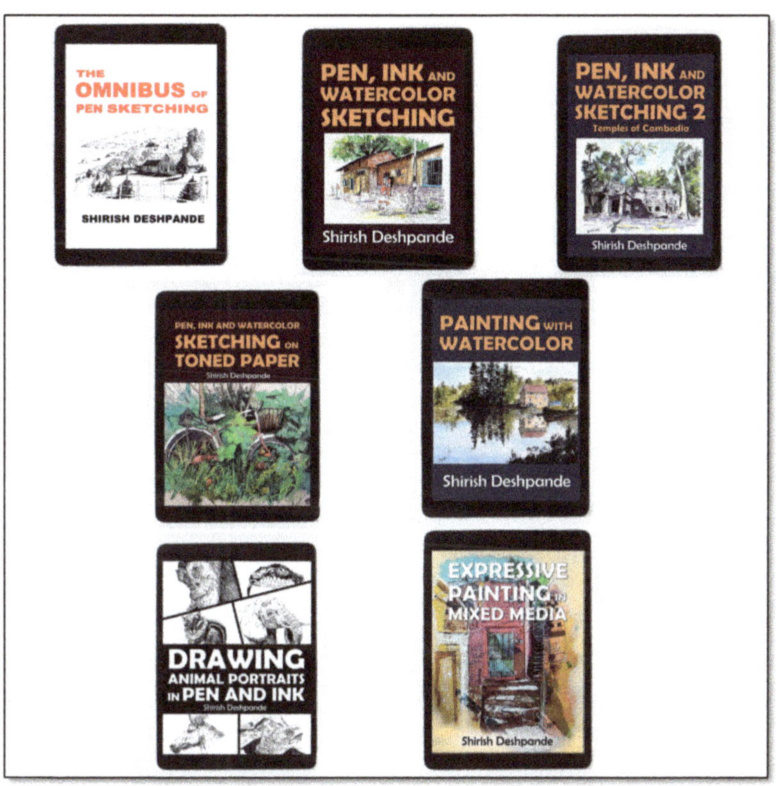

Paperbacks

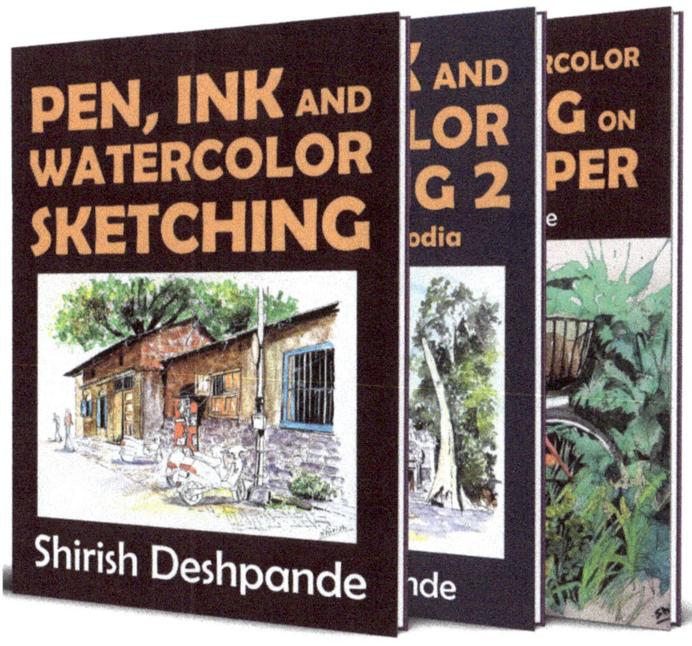